MW00678630

TOKYO 2020
CANDIDATE CITY
2020年オリンピック・
パラリンピックを日本で!
ANRAKUTEI
ANRAKUTEI
ANRAKUTEI
味しんご
OISHINGO
4F
焼肉店
湖南菜館
4F
レンタルルーム
3F
エデン
Eden
nom.²
5F
4F
3F
Party Space
リフレッシュ
星のしずく
カラオケ
747
麻雀
DVD・VID
コロッケクラブ
タイ古式マッサージ
2F
St. James
湖南菜館
4F
ゲーム
メンズ

TOKYO

CAPITAL OF COOL

ROB GOSS

TUTTLE Publishing

Tokyo | Rutland, Vermont | Singapore

CONTENTS

CHAPTER 1
Introducing Tokyo 6
The Capital of Cool 9
The World's Ultimate City 10
From Edo to Tokyo: The Shogun's Capital 14
Tokyo's Colorful Festivals 18
Tokyo's Cutting-Edge Architecture 22
The World's Trendiest City 26
A Foodie Mecca 30

CHAPTER 2
Central Tokyo 34
Tokyo's Central Districts 37
Tokyo Station and Marunouchi 38
The Imperial Palace 40
Ginza 44
Tsukiji Market and Kabuki-za 46
Hamarikyu Garden 48

CHAPTER 3
Eastern and Northern Tokyo 50
Tokyo's Eastern and Northern Districts 53
Akihabara 54
Asakusa and Senso-ji 56
Tokyo Skytree and Asahi Beer Hall 58
The Sumida River 60
Ueno 62
Kiyosumi Garden 64

CHAPTER 4

Southern Tokyo *66*

Tokyo's Southern Districts *69*

Roppongi *70*

Tokyo Tower *74*

Daikanyama, Ebisu, Meguro and Shinagawa *76*

Odaiba *78*

CHAPTER 5

Western Tokyo *80*

Tokyo's Western Districts *83*

Omotesando and Harajuku *84*

Meiji Shrine and Yoyogi Park *88*

Shibuya *90*

Shinjuku *94*

CHAPTER 6

Around Tokyo *98*

Side Trips Around Tokyo *101*

Yokohama *102*

Kamakura *106*

Hakone and Mount Fuji *110*

Nikko *114*

Photo Credits *118*

INTRODUCING
TOKYO

Tokyo
EASTERN AND NORTHERN TOKYO
WESTERN TOKYO
CENTRAL TOKYO
SOUTHERN TOKYO
Senkawa
Kanamecho
Ikebukuro
Otsuka
Sugamoshinden
Toei Mita Line
Komagome
Sugamo
Yamanote Line
Nambuku Line
Tabata
Shinmika-washima
Arakawa Kuyakushomae
Arakawa-itchumae
Mikawashima
Minamisenju
SHIOIRI (PARK)
Higashinagasaki
Toei Oedo Line
Shiinamachi
Ochiaiminami nagasaki
Mejiro-dori
JR Yamanote Line
Mejiro
Kishibojinmae
H.Yonchome
Shinotsuka
Marunouchi Line
Sengoku
Hongo-dori
Nishinippori
Nippori
Chiyoda Line
Jaban Line
Minowabashi
Minowa
Shirahige-bashi
Meiji-dori
Nakai
Shin Mejiro-dori
Shimoochiai
Takadanobaba
Gokokuji
Myogadani
Hakusan
Honko-magome
Sendagi
Todaimae
Nezu
Uguisudani
Ueno District
UENO
Hibiya Line
Kototoi-dori
Sumida River
Sumidagawa River
Senso-ji Temple
Asakusa
Hikifune
Keisei-Hikifune
Tobu Kameido Line
Ochiai
Waseda
Edgawabashi
Kasuga-dori
Kasuga
Korakuen
Inaricho
Ginza Line
Tawaramachi
Tokyo Skytree
Oshiage
Asahi Beer Hall
Honjoazubashi
Higashinakano
Okubo-dori
Fukutoshin Line
Tozai Line
Kagurazaka
Shin-okachimachi
Ueno-hirokoji
Toei Asakusa Line
Hanzomon Line
Asakusa-dori
TOYAMA HEIGHTS
Suidobashi
Suehirocho
Kanda Myojin
Akihabara
Kuramae
Okubo
Shin-Okubo
Higashi-shinjuku
Wakama-tsucho
Ushigome-yanagicho
Ushigome-kagurazaka
Iidabashi
Ochanomizu
Asakusabashi
KINSHI-KOEN (PARK)
Nakanosakaue
Kanda-gawa
SHINJUKU
Shinjuku-sanchome
Toei Shinjuku Line
Akebonobashi
Ichigaya
Jinbocho
Kudanshita
Iwamotocho
Ryogoku
Sobu Line
Kinshicho
Keiyo Rd
Tochomae
Shinjuku
Nishi-shinjuku-gochome
Shinjuku-gyoenmae
Yotsuya Sanchome
Yotsuya
Kojimachi
Hanzomon
Imperial Palace
Ogawamachi
Awajicho
Kanda
Kodenmacho
Higashi-nihonbashi
Morishitashirakawa
SARUEONSHI-KOEN (PARK)
Kikukawa
Sumiyoshi
Shinnihonbashi
Ningyocho
Hamacho
Otemachi
Hatagaya
Hatsudai
Sangubashi
Yoyogi
Sendagaya
Shinanomachi
Tokyo Station
Nihonbashi
Kayabacho
Suitengumae
Kiyosumi-shirakawa
Kiyosumi Gerden
Meiji Shrine
Kokuritsu Kyogijo
Nagatacho
Akasaka-mitsuke
Kokkagijidomae
Nijubashimae
Kyobashi
Takaracho
Hatchobori
Yoyogi-uehara
Yoyogikoen
Yoyogi Park
Harajuku
Hanzomon Line
Aoyama Itchome
Akasaka
Tameike-sanno
Kasumigaseki
Hibiya
Ginza
Shintomicho
Monzennakacho
Kiba
Toyocho
Inokashira-dori
Meijijingu-mae
Omotesando
Gaienmae
Nogizaka
Roppongi
Chiyoda Line
Toranomon
Toei Mita Line
Ginza Line
Tukiji-shijo
Tsukiji
Kachidoki-bashi
Etchujima
Tsukishima
KOMABA-KOEN (PARK)
Shibuya
ROPPONGI
Roppongi Ichome
Kamiyacho
Onarimon
Shimbashi
Shiodome
Tsukiji and Kabuki-za
Hamarikyu Garden
Yurakucho Line
Komabatodaimae
Shinsen
SHIBUYA
Tokyo Tower
Zojo-ji Temple
Daimon
Kachidoki
Shiomi
Toyosu
Ikejiriohashi
ARISUGAWA-NOMIYA-KOEN (PARK)
Hiro-o
Azabujuban
Akabanebashi
Shibakoen
Hinode Takeshiba
Keiyo Line
YUMENOS KOEN (PARK)
Daikanyama
Ebisu
Hibiya Line
Mita
Tamachi
SETAGAYA (PARK)
Nakameguro
Shirokane-takanawa
Tatsumi
Shibaura-futo
Tokyo Bay
Yamate-dori
Meguro-gawa
Rainbow Bridge
Shinonome
Yutenji
Komazawa-dori
Shirokanedai
Sengakuji
Toei Asakusa Line
Ariake
Kokusai-Tenjijo-seimon
Gakugeidaigaku
Meguro
Takanawadai
Shinagawa
SHINAGAWA
Odaiba
Odaibakaihinkoen
Port of Tokyo
Sunamachiminami
Meguro-dori
Gotanda
Tokyoteleport
Rinkai-shinkotsu Line
Yurikamome Train Base
Tokyu Toyoko Line
RINSHINOMORI-KOEN (PARK)
Tokyu Meguro Line
Fudomae
Osaki-hirokoji
Osaki
Kitashi-nagawa
Tennozu Isle
Daiba
Aomi
Fune-no kagakukan
FUNENO-KAGAKUKAN
1 km
1 mile
scale 1 : 70 000
Musashikoyama
Togoshiginza
Togoshi
Keikyu Line
Shinbanba
Tokyo-ko Tunnel
Telecomcenter
N

THE CAPITAL OF COOL

Tokyo is a city of wonderful and often bemusing contrasts and contradictions. Traditional Japanese gardens and ancient temples sit at ease in the shadows of towering skyscrapers. The conservative suits that fill the subway at rush hour can often be punctuated by a colorful kimono. There is a set way of doing almost everything, yet fashion-wise absolutely anything can go. The list goes on. The Japanese like to think of themselves as being unique (sometimes a touch too much), but thanks to a patchwork of districts, each with its own personality, not to mention an unorchestrated blend of new, old, home-grown and imported, their capital is undoubtedly one of the most distinctive cities on the planet.

TOKYO

THE WORLD'S ULTIMATE CITY

Metropolis. Mega city. Call Tokyo what you will, but there is no disputing the status of Japan's capital as one of the world's great cities. Just over 13 million people call Tokyo home, nearly 35 million if you count the neighboring prefectures of Kanagawa, Saitama and Chiba, which with Tokyo make up the most common definition of the Greater Tokyo area, an unbroken urban sprawl that spreads mile upon mile west, north and east from the center of Tokyo.

The crowds, energy, lights and fashions of Shibuya at night epitomize modern Tokyo.

Tokyo's current place in the world, only 70 years after the city was all but decimated by war (90 after it was leveled by an earthquake), is nothing short of miraculous. From a business perspective, the Tokyo Stock Exchange has become one of the main financial hubs in Asia, while Tokyo also competes with Hong Kong, Singapore and Shanghai as the Asian base for many multinational corporations, not to mention being home to major Japanese corporations with global reach and recognition, companies that have forged a reputation for cutting-edge and precision technology and efficiency.

In a sporting sense, after rebuilding from World War II, the Tokyo Olympics in 1964 was one of the first opportunities for Tokyo to show the world it was back. Since then, Tokyo has become the host venue for the 2002 World Cup, held jointly with South Korea, as well as a regular host of football's Confederation Cup and many other major sporting events across a range of disciplines. And with the awarding of the 2020 Olympics and Paralympics, Tokyo is now gearing up to once again be the focus of the world's greatest sporting celebrations.

Culturally, traditional Japanese arts and craft have long been appreciated and influential overseas but, emanating from Tokyo, so too has modern Japanese culture. On the back of *manga* (comic books), *anime* (animation), video games and related products, Akihabara is the center point of a globally reaching *otaku* (geek) culture. Tokyo also has one of the world's most vibrant contemporary art scenes, highlighted by major annual events such as the

LEFT Japan is a pioneer in the field of robotics. Honda's humanoid Asimo robot, pictured here performing at the Miraikan in Odaiba (page 78), can talk, dance and even kick a football. Do not be surprised to soon see robots working as home helpers, receptionists and performing many other roles in Tokyo.

RIGHT The latest technology on display. Japan's home electronics makers produce world-leading products, which you can check out in megastores like Yodobashi and Bic Camera or in the home electronics district of Akihabara (page 54).

RIGHT In Harajuku, you will see that style-wise anything goes in Tokyo. **BELOW RIGHT** Fashionable districts like Shibuya and Roppongi have some of the best clubs in Asia.

Roppongi Art Night and the biannual Design Festa, the world's largest freestyle art fair.

But one thing that differentiates Japan from other "world cities" is the population breakdown. For better or worse, and despite people from 190 different nations living in Tokyo, Tokyo remains predominantly Japanese. Of the 13.2 million people living in Tokyo, only around 3 percent are non-Japanese (compare that to over 30 percent in London or more than 35 percent in New York), the majority of that figure being Korean and Chinese nationals, many of whom were born in Japan.

TOP AND ABOVE The Tokyo Stock Exchange in the Nihombashi district is one of Asia's main trading venues.
ABOVE RIGHT Despite Tokyo's reputation for high-rise, high-tech and neon, tradition often punctuates the modern metropolis. Here, women wear kimono as they enjoy the spring cherry blossoms.
RIGHT A helicopter cruise takes in Tokyo Tower and sprawling central Tokyo. For the especially well-heeled, helicopter taxis also run from Narita Airport to the city center.

RIGHT Relaxing after work at the *yakitori* (grilled chicken) restaurants underneath the rail tracks by Yurakucho Station. Japan has a very rich and varied culinary heritage of its own, but Tokyo is also a truly global culinary city. With an estimated 90,000–100,000 licensed eateries, Tokyo's dining scene stretches from Korean, Chinese and Southeast Asian to European, Middle Eastern and beyond.

ABOVE The subway whizzes by. Tokyo's spider web of a train and subway network runs with incredible efficiency, only stopping (or just slowing) briefly when typhoons hit or when somebody commits suicide on the tracks.
LEFT If you want to experience Tokyo's crowds first hand, try a rush-hour train or the Shibuya Crossing at night.

FROM EDO TO TOKYO: THE SHOGUN'S CAPITAL

In 1590, 13 years before unifying Japan and becoming the first of the Edo-era shoguns, Tokugawa Ieyasu chose the town of Edo as his base of power. At the time, what is now Tokyo was not much more than marshland and estuaries centered around a small and ageing fortress, but by the time the Edo era had come to an end in 1868, Ieyasu's capital had become the world's largest city.

At the heart of Edo was the Tokugawa's Edo Castle, originally built in 1457 by a *daimyo* (lord) called Ota Dokan, but then transformed by Tokugawa Ieyasu and subsequent shoguns into what was reputedly the largest castle in the world in its day. At its peak, its inner compound was some 8 kilometers in diameter, the outer compound 16 kilometers, and at its heart was a castle donjon with a 50-meter-high, five-tiered façade. During 260 years of Tokugawa rule, the castle was a potent symbol of power that remained unbreached, only succumbing to fires that frequently wreaked havoc on Edo.

During the relative stability and peace of Tokugawa rule, Edo grew rapidly both in size and economic strength. By the early 1700s, the population had reached one million, and to find space for the ever-growing populace hills were leveled, marshes reclaimed and estuaries filled. In Dokan's day, areas such as Ginza and Nihombashi would have been under water, but during the Edo era they would both begin to flourish, Ginza initially as the location for the shogunate's main silver mint and Nihombashi as a commercial center and the point from which all distances from Tokyo would be measured. Edo grew in all directions, even taking large chunks out of Tokyo Bay, but even amid such rapid growth the rigid social lines of Tokugawa rule were never blurred. The samurai classes had their parts of town and each level of merchant and worker had theirs. Today, in some parts of Tokyo you can still see distinctions between the "high city" of the samurai and the "low city" of the common man.

LEFT *Gogatsu ningyo* (lit. May dolls) are an example of how tradition still underpins modern Tokyo life. Displayed on Kodomo-no-hi, or Children's Day (May 5th), by families with sons, these sets are said to bring good health and happiness for boys. Ornate dolls for girls are also displayed each year as part of the Hina-matsuri (Doll Festival) in March.
ABOVE A traditional dance performance.

RIGHT Many major traditional festivals, such as the autumn and spring festivals at Tosho-gu Shrine in Nikko and Tsurugaoka Hachiman-gu Shrine in Kamakura, feature processions in historical costumes like this samurai armor.

ABOVE The classic view of the Imperial Palace (page 40) in central Tokyo combines the Fushimi Yagura guard tower and Nijubashi Bridge.
LEFT Tradition, though important, can be tinkered with, especially when it comes to fashion. In this case, *zori* sandals meet platforms.

LEFT (INSET) A *ukiyo-e* (woodblock print) depicting an Edo-era *kabuki* actor.
LEFT Decorative *hagoita* at the annual Hagoita-Ichi fair by Senso-ji Temple in Asakusa. A *hagoita* is a flat wooden racket used for playing the traditional New Year's game *hanetsuki*, although ones like these are used as good luck charms.
BELOW You can still see rickshaws in Asakusa, although only as a tourist attraction nowadays.

With Tokugawa rule ended by the Meiji Restoration of 1868, Edo went through a series of dramatic changes. When the 17-year-old Meiji Emperor moved from Kyoto to briefly take up residence in Edo Castle (it burnt down in 1873 and the site is now home to the current Imperial Palace), he renamed Edo the "eastern capital", Tokyo. The Meiji Government also set about modernizing Japan. With help of foreign expertise previously kept out of the country by Edo-era isolation policy, Japan developed its railways and industries. From the 1880s onward, much of central Tokyo also underwent a Western-style facelift, European architects and later their Japanese students erecting brick buildings. Horse-drawn carriages replaced rickshaws. Gas street lights appeared. The Meiji Emperor even took to wearing Western clothing. Tokugawa's former power base had become the modern mega city of its day.

ABOVE LEFT Dolls on a souvenir stall.
ABOVE CENTER A statue of the legendary 14th-century samurai Kusunoki Masahige near the Imperial Palace.
ABOVE A glimpse of old Edo courtesy of the master *ukiyo-e* artist Hiroshige.

ABOVE Performing the tea ceremony. *Sado* or *Chado*, as it is most commonly known in Japanese, is still a popular and very well-respected pastime.
RIGHT Decorative saké barrels (*kazaridaru*) at Meiji Jingu Shrine. Although the ones on display are always empty, shrines often use saké in parts of their rituals.

TOKYO'S COLORFUL FESTIVALS

Year round, Tokyo's calendar is marked by festivals of all shapes and guises, from local street fairs to ancient parades and from midsummer fireworks displays to seasonal flower festivals, a collection of *matsuri* (festivals) woven into the fabric of Tokyo life.

In early spring, the focus of the city's festivities is the fleeting wave of cherry blossom (*sakura*) that arrives in Tokyo in late March and early April as it sweeps northeast over Japan, with it signaling the start of *hanami* (cherry blossom viewing) parties and picnics in parks and alongside river banks all over the city. In Ueno Park, *hanami* manifests itself in thousands of saké- and beer-fueled parties on a sea of blue tarpaulin picnic sheets under delicate pink blossoms, while in other places the viewing is a more peaceful, contemplative affair, the lawns of Shinjuku Gyoen and a row boat on the picturesque Chidorigafuchi moat by the Imperial Palace being two of the most attractive and tranquil viewing spots in Tokyo.

As spring begins to warm with the approach of early summer, the first of Tokyo's grand festivals begin. Taking place in odd-numbered years, the Kanda Matsuri in mid-May features

OPPOSITE Dancing in the streets at one of Tokyo's numerous summer festivals.
LEFT The procession of samurai at the Tosho-gu Grand Spring Festival.
ABOVE Picnicking under spring cherry blossoms. A favorite annual event in Japan, *hanami* (blossom viewing parties) take place all over Tokyo when the *sakura* is in bloom.
RIGHT Paper lanterns at temple and shrine festivals can look mystical but often just bear the names of people who have given donations.

processions of men in Edo-era costumes, bearers of *mikoshi* (portable shrines) and priests on horseback, while a week or so later the Sanja Matsuri in Asakusa attracts almost two million onlookers who come to watch hollering teams of bearers bounce highly decorative *mikoshi* through the teeming streets in honor of the 7th-century founders of Asakusa's Senso-ji Temple and take in the parades of floats and food stalls.

When the heat and humidity of summer arrives in July and August, *matsuri* madness reaches its peak. Illuminating Tokyo's eastern skies on the final Saturday of July, the Sumidagawa Hanabi Taikai is the largest of dozens of summer *hanabi taikai* (fireworks displays) that take place in Tokyo, in this case with 20,000 rockets painting a rainbow of colors above the Sumida River. Despite the often oppressive heat, outdoor dance events are popular too, especially August's Koenji Awa Odori (a modern-day offshoot of the centuries-old Awa Odori folk dance festival held in Tokushima Prefecture), which sees 12,000 dancers split into hundreds of colorfully dressed male and female troupes take to the sun-baked streets of Koenji to perform Awa folk dances to up-tempo rhythms and a pulsating mix of drums, flutes and traditional stringed instruments.

In Autumn, the number of *matsuri* taking place in Tokyo begins to drop off from the summer peak, although major traditional parades and displays of horseback archery take place in both Kamakura and Nikko as part of Tsurugaoka Hachimangu Shrine's and Toshogu Shrine's seasonal celebrations, each offering a window on important periods in Japan's feudal past and a chance to enjoy some of the traditions that accompany almost every Japanese festival—the aromas and flavors of the street food, the colorful silk kimono or cotton *yukata* that accent the crowds, the simple fair games for children.

ABOVE Fireworks displays (*hanabi taikai*) are a summer institution all over the country, including Tokyo. For a major event like the Sumida River Fireworks in late July, somewhere in the region of half a million onlookers head to the banks of the Sumida to watch some 20,000 rockets being set off.

LEFT AND FAR LEFT Processions in historic dress are a feature of many major shrine festivals.

RIGHT It is very common to get dressed up for Shichi-go-san (lit. seven, five, three), a rite-of-passage festival in November for girls aged three and seven and boys aged five.

BELOW The Asakusa Samba Carnival. Not all festivals are bathed in Japanese tradition.

BELOW It would not be a festival without the food stalls. *Yakitori* (grilled chicken), *yakisoba* (fried noodles), *okonomiyaki* (a kind of thick savory pancake), grilled fish, cotton candy and *kakigori* (shaved ice) are all common finds at a festival.

ARCH

TOKYO'S CUTTING-EDGE ARCHITECTURE

A mish-mash of architectural styles coupled with an unshackled approach to urban planning has given Tokyo a distinctive appearance. Like many major cities, Tokyo has its gray urban sprawl, but no other city punctuates the mundane quite like Japan's capital. With a blank canvas afforded them by a combination of loose planning regulations, adventurous developers and the freedom given by the Japanese acceptance of impermanence, Japanese architects have created pockets of architectural wonder and, occasionally, architectural bewilderment, in the process names such as Toyo Ito, Tadao Ando, Kisho Kurokawa and Kenzo Tange becoming internationally acclaimed for their distinctive, ground-breaking styles.

To pluck a few examples from the air, conceptual architect Toyo Ito's Mikimoto Ginza 2 Building, said to be inspired by jewelry boxes (Mikimoto, after all, is Japan's most prestigious jeweler) and punctuated by striking cell-like windows, is one reason Ito won the prestigious 2013 Pritzker Prize for Architecture. Ando's Omotesando Hills mall, built in 2006, features a six-level atrium that reaches three stories above ground and three below, with a spiraling ramp connecting the different levels. Tange's Fuji TV headquarters, which is defined by a titanium-paneled silver sphere that appears to have lodged itself into the giant walkways connecting the structure's two main buildings, is the defining sight on the man-made island of Odaiba.

Contemporary foreign architects have also left their mark, none more so than Phillipe Starck's Asahi Beer Hall, which combines a stout building with a polished black granite façade on top of which sits a 300-ton golden

LEFT The distinctive "ball" that appears to have fallen and lodged itself into the Kenzo Tange-designed Fuji TV offices on Odaiba. RIGHT Another of Tange's works is the Mode Gakuen Cocoon Tower in Shinjuku, which houses a fashion college, IT school and medical college. The cocoon design is said to symbolize the nurturing of the students inside.

RIGHT The Tokyo Skytree, at 634 meters, is the second tallest structure in the world. **FAR RIGHT** Designer Rafael Vinoly shaped the outside of the Tokyo International Forum like an elongated boat, while the cavernous interiors are defined by swooping steel trusses and glass panels.

LEFT The Kenzo Tange-designed Tokyo Metropolitan Government Building (aka Tocho) in Shinjuku, which opened in 1991. At 243 meters, the twin-towered building was Tokyo's tallest until Tokyo Midtown was completed in 2006.

RIGHT (INSET) Mikimoto Ginza 2 in Ginza is home to jewelers Mikimoto. Acclaimed architect Toyo Ito used a simple rectangular shape to fit the limited space and concentrated on creating a memorable façade, which has a honeycomb effect from multiple irregularly placed windows.

RIGHT The Prada Aoyoma building, designed by architects Herzog & de Meuron. Many of Tokyo's most striking structures have been built for major fashion brands.

"flame" with a taller structure that is designed to look like a glass of chilled lager. More high-tech is the Chanel store in Ginza, housed in a 10-story building designed in 2004 by Peter Marino that uses 70,000 light-emitting diodes on its exterior walls to frequently change its appearance.

The 2000s also saw the rise of the urban complex. The towering Roppongi Hills and Tokyo Midtown, often described as cities within the city, have combined to transform the Roppongi area into one of Tokyo's most fashionable and cosmopolitan addresses, just as Ando's Omotesando Hills mall redefined one side of Omotesando-dori. And even more recent than those has come a structure that you could not miss, even if you wanted to, in the shape of Tokyo Skytree, a 634-meter-tall broadcast tower-cum-tourist attraction that now looms large over eastern Tokyo.

RIGHT The AO Building in Aoyama and its "twisted" tower house luxury fashion brands, cafés, restaurants and interior design stores.

BELOW RIGHT The National Art Center in Roppongi.

BELOW CENTER The Nakagin Capsule Tower is a retro classic. Built in 1972 and designed by Kisho Kurosawa, the mixed-use residential and office tower comprising 140 small capsules is a rare example of Metabolism Movement architecture.

BELOW LEFT The Audi Forum Tokyo, aka "The Iceberg", in Shibuya Ward was designed by Tokyo-based Creative Designers International.

TRENDIEST CITY

THE WORLD'S TRENDIEST CITY

Teen trends and fashions move like ever-shifting sands in Tokyo. One minute platform shoes are in, the next it is crop tops. One season neon is the new black, and then pink is the new neon; or tie-dye is suddenly in vogue after a month or two of nothing but stripes. The only constants are where the styles are born—the streets of Shibuya and Harajuku.

In Shibuya, in boutique-filled buildings like 109, new youth concepts and trends are unleashed on Tokyo before spreading out across Japan, often out of date in Shibuya by the time the rest of the country has caught on. Along streets like Takeshita-dori in Harajuku it is a similar story, while in Akihabara, an area known for its home electronics stores and *anime* and *manga* shops, *otaku* (geek) teens show off incredible cosplay fashions that can range from dressing up as comic

ABOVE No other part of Tokyo is as colorful as Shibuya (page 90) on Halloween.
BELOW Posing on the street for amateur photographers in Akihabara (page 54).

Other world cities might argue against Tokyo being the "trendiest", but Tokyo undisputedly has an amazing range and variety of fashions, from cosplay (**FAR LEFT**) to glitzy (**LEFT**) and simple but trendy fashions offered by popular brands such as Uniqlo (**ABOVE**). Fashion-wise, anything can and does go in Tokyo.

ABOVE AND TOP You get a real mix of styles in the shops and streets of Shibuya (page 90). TOP CENTER Harajuku (page 84) is the place to check out the latest fashion trends among teens and young adults.

book characters to donning a blood-splattered gothic nurse look.

Some styles, of course, persist. *Gyaru* (a word derived from "gal") street fashion, which is characterized by bleached or dyed hair, highly decorated nails and heavy make-up such as dark eyeliner and false eyelashes, has been dominant since it first came to prominence in areas like Shibuya and Harajuku in the 1970s. Yet, even that has branched off into numerous sub-*gyaru* styles.

Hime-gyaru, for example, favor a princess look with pink or pastel dresses adorned with lace and bows. The *ganguro* look that was big in the 1990s and early 2000s brought dark fake tans and outrageously bleached hair to the basic *gyaru* style, and then warped into the *manba* and *yamanba* styles—look out for the same fake tans but with a mix of bleached and neon hair and heavy white make-up above or below the eyes. Confused? Unless you are a teen, you should be.

Some themes last too. Cuteness (*kawaii*) never seems to go out of fashion, whether reflected in the cuddly character goods and sparkly trinkets high schoolers have hanging from their ubiquitous cell phones or the distinctive mannerisms some seem to affect, be that pouting or raising the pitch of their voice to dog whistle range. Whatever you think of the fashions and styles, you have to tip your hat to Tokyo's youth for one thing—they are not afraid to express themselves and Tokyo is a much more vibrant and dynamic city for it.

ABOVE Among the suits and Western-style fashions, traditional clothing like these kimono are still a fairly regular sight. On Coming of Age Day, on the second Monday of January, woman aged 20 celebrate adulthood by wearing kimono like the ones pictured, with a fake fur stole. Some people wear kimono to events such as weddings, while others working in traditional stores or restaurants might wear them to work.
LEFT Outside the Louis Vuitton store in Ginza (page 44). No matter how long or deep Japan goes into recession, the high-end fashion brands still remain in demand.

A FOODIE MECCA

From simple *ramen* to sublime *kaiseki-ryori*, from kebab trucks to Michelin-starred French cuisine, the breadth and quality of food in Tokyo has made the city a gourmands delight, a city many call the culinary capital of the world.

To put Tokyo's culinary clout into numbers, there are somewhere near 100,000 licensed eating establishments in Tokyo, the top end of which have garnered more than twice as many Michelin stars as any other city in the world. At last count, Tokyo's 281 starred restaurants were way ahead of the 70 in Paris and 67 in New York.

To judge Tokyo simply by its plushest restaurants, however, does not do the city and Japan's culinary heritage justice. Tokyo is the foodie capital of the world, not just for its high end but because of its incredible epicurean depth and breadth, across which chefs from each culinary walk of life tend to share the same level of craftsmanship and dedication, be they focused on perfecting a single broth and noodle combination or creating seasonal delicacies delivered with artistic aplomb and traditional elegance.

Specialization is a defining trait, from affordable restaurants that serve only soba noodles to highly refined establishments where elaborate courses can revolve around a multitude of uses of tofu,

OPPOSITE LEFT Lanterns outside a restaurant often highlight the type of food and drink on the menu. This particular place has (left to right) *oden*, *soba*, seasonal *kushikatsu* and *shochu*.
OPPOSITE RIGHT Restaurants in Tokyo do not only cover the full range of Japanese cuisines but also European, Chinese, Korean, Southeast Asian and almost everything else.
RIGHT Fresh *sashimi* (slices of raw fish).
FAR RIGHT A street vendor cooks up *yakisoba* (fried noodles).
BELOW Casual *yakitori* (grilled chicken) restaurants in Yurakucho, a stone's throw from the plush Ginza district.

TOP Fast food the traditional way. Counter-only places like this often offer great tasting food at reasonable prices for a quick lunch or dinner. Looking at the signs, this one does a super cheap 500 yen lunch box of grilled eel on rice. ABOVE A teppanyaki restaurant. As with many sushi and tempura restaurants, one of the great things with teppanyaki (besides the hotplate-fried meat, seafood and vegetables) is being able to watch the chefs prepare your food up close.

and from low-budget *kaitenzushi* restaurants, where customers pluck the *nigiri* from conveyor belts, to $200-plus a head *sushi-ya* in well-heeled areas like Ginza and Roppongi.

Some areas even specialize. The Okubo area, next to Shinjuku, has Tokyo's best selection and biggest concentration of Korean restaurants. Nearby Hyakunincho is best for "ethnic" (meaning Southeast Asian) cuisine. Yokohama has Chinatown. More cosmopolitan locales, such as Roppongi, Aoyama and Omotesando, are the places to look for both traditional high-end dining and innovative modern takes on Japanese cuisine, not to mention international fare of all kinds.

In less fashionable areas, Shimbashi is great for boisterous after work *izakaya*, although such traditional watering holes are found everywhere. Ryogoku, home to Japan's main sumo stadium, is known for restaurants serving *chanko nabe*, the hearty hotpot of meat, vegetables and seafood eaten by sumo wrestlers. The Tsukishima area is known for a Tokyo oddity called *monjayaki*, a runny batter containing a mix of chopped vegetables, meat or seafood that is then grilled into a sticky mess on hotplates built into each table. The variety is such you could spend a month in Tokyo trying a different lunch and dinner every day and still barely have scratched the surface.

BELOW TOP Fresh produce on display at the outer market area of Tsukiji Market, which provides restaurants in Tokyo, from high-end sushi bars in Ginza to back-street *izakaya*, with much of their seafood.
BELOW CENTER An assortment of *sashimi* (slices of raw fish) served with freshly grated *wasabi* (for mixing with soy sauce as a dip) on decorative bamboo leaves.
BELOW BOTTOM A sushi chef puts the final touches to a serving of *mushi ebi* (steamed shrimp sushi).

ABOVE Skewers of *yakitori* on the grill.
LEFT Fish cooking on an open hearth. Dishes like these are a perfect match for beer and saké.
BELOW At a sushi restaurant.

CENTRAL TOKYO

KUDAN-KITA
Yushukan War Museum
Yasukuni Shrine
KUDAN-MINAMI
Kudanshita
National Showa Memorial Museum
Shinjuku Line
Yasukuni-dori
Jimbocho
KANDA-OGAWAMACHI
Hanzomon Line
Yasukuni-dori
Shin-Ochanomizu
Ogawamachi
Awajicho
Kanda-tsukasamachi
Kanda-tacho
Kanda
Iwamotocho
HIGASHI-KANDA
IWAMOTOCHO
NIHOMBASHI-BAKUROCHO
Bakurocho
Kita-no-maru-koen
KITA-NO-MARU PARK
Science Museum
HITOTSUBASHI
Mita Line
KANDA-NISHIKICHO
Chiyoda Line
Hongo-dori
UCHI-KANDA
Kanda Keisatsu-
Kanda Kajicho
Ginza Line
Hibiya Line
Nihombashi-kodenmacho
Sobu Line
Bakuro Yokohama
Higashi-nihombashi
Asakusa Line
Bijutsukan Kogeikan (Crafts Gallery)
Sanbancho
Uchibori-dori
Shuro E'way Loop Line
National Museum of Modern Art
Takebashi
Uchibori-dori
Mita & Chiyoda Line
Kodenmacho
Shin-nihombashi
Nihombashi-hisamatsucho
Nihombashi-odenmacho
Nihombashi-honcho
Nihombashi-tomizawacho
Ichibancho
Edo Castle Ruin
NINO-MARU AREA
OTEMACHI
Nihombashi-hongokucho
Mitsukoshi-mae
Nihombashi-horidomecho
The Imperial Palace East Garden
Museum of Imperial Collections
Otemachi
Communications Museum
Mitsui Memorial Museum
Nihombashi-kobunacho
Ningyocho
NIHOMBASHI HAMACHO
Hanzomon
JCII Camera Museum
KOKYO
FUKIAGE IMPERIAL GARDEN
HON-MARU AREA
Eitai-dori
Currency Museum
Nihombashi-muromachi
NIHOMBASHI NINGYOCHO
Hanzomon Line
Mitsukoshimae
Nihombashi-koamicho
Visitor Center
Chiyoda
IMPERIAL PALACE GROUNDS
The Imperial Palace
Kite Museum
Nihombashi
Suitengumae
HIRAKAWACHO
Kokyo-gaien
Nihombashi Kabutocho
Base Gallery
NIHOMBASHI KAKIGARACHO
Tokyo
Tokyo Station
Fushimi Yagura Tower
THE IMPERIAL PALACE OUTER GARDEN
Nijubashi-mae
YAESU
Eita-dori
Kayabacho
Chiyoda
Nijubashi Bridge
Uchibori-dori
MARUNOUCHI
Sotobori-dori
Showa-dori
Bridgestone Museum of Art
KAYABACHO
Hakozaki
Aoyama-dori
Nagatacho
Parliamentary Museum
Marunouchi My Plaza
Mitsubishi Ichigokan Museum
KYOBASHI
NIHOMBASHI
Nihombashi River
NAGATACHO
KASUMIGASEKI PARK
Sakuradamon
Yurakucho Line
Idemitsu Museum of Arts
Tokyo (Keiyo Line)
Yaesu-dori
Tozai Line
Imperial Theater
Tokyo Int'l Forum
Kyobashi
National Diet Bldg Kokkai Gijido
Marunouchi Line
KASUMIGASEKI
Hibiya
Yurakucho
Takaracho
HATCHOBORI
Hatchobori
SHINKAWA
Kokkai-gijidomae
Kasumigaseki
Hibiya Park
YURAKUCHO
Muji
Ginza-Itchome
Police Museum
National Film Center
Kajibashi-dori
Hibiya-koen
Printemps
Zara
Cartier
Ginza Yanagi-dori
Tameike-sanno
Kokkai-gijidomae
SUKIYA-BASHI CROSSING
Mikimoto Pearls
Bvlgari
Matsuya
Ginza Chuo-dori
SINTOMI
IRIFUNE
MINATO
Wako
Ginza Noh Theater
Kyukyudo Bldg
GINZA CROSSING
Mitsukoshi Dept. Store
Sotobori-dori
Toranomon
UCHISAIWAICHO
Chanel
Uniqlo
Ginza
Higashi-ginza
Kabuki-za
Shintomicho
Uchisaiwaicho
TORANOMON
Sakurada-dori
Zara
H&M
Akashicho
Okura Museum
NISHI-SHIMBASHI
Mita Line
Shimbashi
Railway History Exhibition Hall
Panasonic Shiodome Museum
Asakusa Line
Tsukiji
Yurakucho Line
TSUKUDA
Shimbashi Embujo Theater
AKATSUKI-KOEN GARDEN
TSUKISHIMA ISLAND
Roppongi-itchome
Hibiya Line
Advertising Museum of Tokyo
Shin-ohashi-dori
Harumi-dori
ATAGO
SHIMBASHI
Tsukiji-shijo
HATOBA PARK
Shio Sight
Shiodome
Oedo Line
Sumida River
Tsukishima
Kamiyacho
NHK Broadcast Museum
Kachi-doki-bashi-no Museum
TSUKISHIMA
Laforet Museum
Hibiya-do ri
HIGASHI-SHIMBASHI
AZABUDAI
Tsukiji Central Wholesale Market
Kiyosumi-dori
Oedo Line
N
Onarimon
Oedo Line
Hamarikyu Garden
SHIBA-KOEN
Kachidoki
Azabu-Mamianacho
Tokyo Tower
Aquarium
Teahouse
500 m
1000 feet
scale 1 : 22 500
HAMAMATSUCHO
Harumi-dori
Sangedatsu-mon
Sakurada-dori
Yurikamome Line
Zojo-ji
Daimon
HIGASHI-AZABU
SHIBA PARK
KACHIDOKI
SHIBA-DAIMON

TOKYO'S CENTRAL DISTRICTS

From the Edo era on, the land that was the site of Edo Castle and is now the location of the current Imperial Palace has effectively functioned as Tokyo's central point. The areas that surround the palace merge traditional wealth and refinement with modern expressions of luxury. Ginza, home to high-end department stores, boutiques and restaurants, is the most obvious expression of central Tokyo's modern luxurious side, while beyond the Imperial Palace itself historic elements are on show in places like Hamarikyu Garden and the Kabuki-za Theater. Connecting the capital with the rest of the country, Tokyo Station manages to combine both old and new, the station's historic façade surrounded by the gleaming skyscrapers of a now rejuvenated business district.

TOKYO STATION AND MARUNOUCHI

Tokyo Station was not the city's first station, nor is it now the busiest or biggest, but at the grand old age of 100, revamped after an extensive five-year ¥50-billion renovation that has both modernized the station and reclaimed some of its historic features, there is no doubt that the station bearing the capital's name is the most iconic *eki* in Japan.

When Tokyo Station opened on December 20, 1914, a short walk from the gardens of the Imperial Palace and with one entrance reserved solely for use by the Imperial family, it was a fairly modest affair, with just four platforms serving two electric and two non-electric trains. In its first year, an average of only 4,000 people a day would board trains here, a hundred times less than now.

With the constant expansion of Japan's railway and subway network, Tokyo Station grew and grew, especially as Japan began to flourish post-war. The first *shinkansen* (bullet train) lines came to the station in 1964, the

BELOW LEFT The restored façade of the original Tokyo Station building opens out on to the skyscrapers of the recently modernized Marunouchi business district, which, in turn, gives way to the Imperial Palace area. With a combination of sleek office spaces, shops, restaurants and cafés, the towering Marunouchi and Shin-Marunouchi buildings, in particular, have helped transform Marunouchi from a once rather staid and dour business area to a fashionable and dynamic business center.
BELOW Part of Tokyo Station's remaining original interior design.
RIGHT The Marunouchi district reflects in one of the outer moats of the Imperial Palace.

BELOW One of the *shinkansen* (bullet train) line platforms at Tokyo Station. In addition to a bewildering number of train and subway lines and platforms, the vast station is also home to numerous shops and eateries. One thing to look out for are the stores between and on the platforms selling *eki-ben* (lit. station lunch boxes), designed for eating on a train journey and ranging from pricey regional specialties to simple quick meals.
BOTTOM Ornamental pines in the outer grounds of the Imperial Palace share the skyline with Marunouchi's office blocks.

same year Tokyo held its first Olympics, and today Tokyo Station is a hub for all *shinkansen* lines heading north to Tohoku and west to Kyoto and beyond, in addition to being served by eight regular JR lines and the Tokyo Metro. Navigating the 20 plus platforms is made all the more tricky by the mass of exits, underground walkways and underground malls in and connected to the station.

Like the city it serves, the station has had some dark moments in its time. In 1921, Prime Minister Hara Takashi was stabbed to death outside the south exit by a right winger upset at Hara's perceived softening of Japan's colonial authority in Asia. In 1938, with fascism rising in Japan, crowds gathered outside the station to welcome a group of Hitlerjugend to Tokyo, and in the war that soon followed parts of the station's original structure—all of which remarkably went unscathed in the great earthquake of 1923—were destroyed in the Allied bombing raids of 1945. Even after peace had returned to Tokyo, there was more major damage sustained in a fire in 1949.

Rectifying that, the recent redevelopment has restored the red brick façade on the Marunouchi side of the station to its original 1914 look, creating a traditional architectural contrast to gleaming skyscrapers such as the office-, store- and restaurant-filled Marunouchi and Shin-Marunouchi buildings that over the past decade have transformed the once drab Marunouchi business district into a modern precinct.

THE IMPERIAL PALACE

You could argue that Tokyo began its rise to prominence at the site where the current Imperial Palace is located. It was here, in 1457, that a samurai called Ota Dokan built a fortified mansion on a hill overlooking an inlet of Tokyo Bay to defend the town of Edo (now Tokyo) that lay around it. Although for a time after Dokan's demise the fortress was abandoned, Tokugawa Ieyasu seized upon the strategic importance of the location when he chose Edo as his power base and built Edo Castle on the same site in the 1590s.

As part of Tokugawa Ieyasu's redevelopment of the site, he filled the inlet and used the newly created land, a large, flat expanse that now forms much of the current palace's outer gardens, to build mansions for his closest allies. He also developed the great moats and walls that still surround the current palace, having his feudal lords bring the giant stones used from Izu peninsula almost 100 kilometers away. It would have been a mighty undertaking, culminating with teams of laborers dragging the stones from the bay to the castle site on sledges, scattering seaweed on the road as they went to lubricate the route. Looking at the scale of the moats and walls, the defenses might seem excessive, but they obviously formed a potent deterrent for, in the 260 years of Tokugawa rule, the castle was never attacked.

OPPOSITE The classic view of the Imperial Palace. In the foreground is the double-arched Nijubashi Bridge, while in the background is the Fushimi Yagura guard tower.
TOP The entrance to the East Gardens of the Imperial Palace.

ABOVE The 14th-century samurai Kusunoki Masahige, who gave his life helping Emperor Go-Daigo defeat the Kamakura shogunate, is commemorated in the palace's outer grounds. Masahige is often held up as the ideal example of the loyal samurai.
RIGHT The Suwa-no-chaya teahouse in the palace's East Gardens.

When Tokugawa rule came to an end in the 1860s, the Emperor Meiji briefly lived in Edo Castle after relocating to the newly named Tokyo from Kyoto. Unfortunately, much of the castle burned down soon after, a fate that was also suffered by the rebuilt palace in World War II. Nowadays, the Imperial Family lives in a modern palace deep within the grounds, but there are still a few remaining original Edo-era structures on the grounds. Most notably for the tour groups that come for photo opportunities in front of the

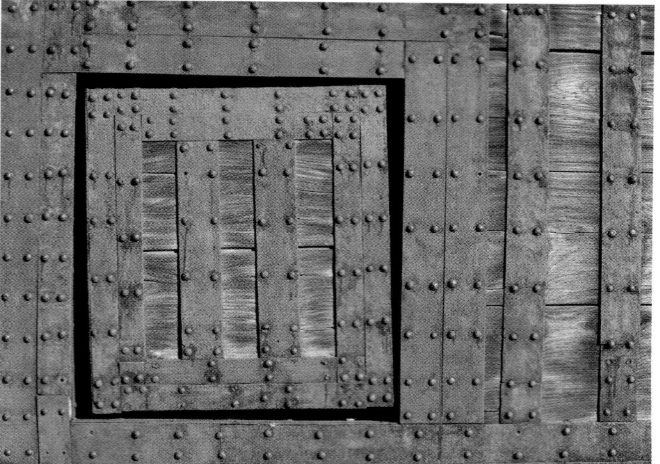

ABOVE The mighty Sakurada-mon Gate. For joggers, the gate is a popular starting and finishing point for an uninterrupted 5-kilometer route that loops around the Imperial Palace. Even as a stroll, the loop helps you get a sense of the scale of the palace's grounds, which are vast for a city where space is usually at such a high premium.
LEFT A window within one of the palace's gates.

moats, the palace's Edo-era Fushimi Yagura tower, which protrudes through dense woods beyond the moat, combines with the stone double arches of the 1888-built Nijubashi Bridge to create one of Tokyo's most distinctive sights.

Not that it would have been so picturesque during the days immediately following the end of World War II. This viewpoint of the palace had taken on an iconic status among the most fanatical members of the Imperial Army during the militaristic 1930s and 1940s, and when the Emperor Hirohito, revered by many as a god, announced Japan's surrender, it was here that many of the beaten army committed ritual suicide to atone for their lost honor.

ABOVE Wadakura Fountain Park, built to commemorate the royal wedding of Emperor Akihito and Empress Michiko (the current emperor and empress) in 1961, is located in the very outer part of the Imperial Palace area.
LEFT The outer grounds of the Imperial Palace.
BELOW A pond within the palace's traditionally landscaped East Gardens. There are more impressive traditional gardens in Tokyo, but the East Gardens still more than warrant a visit, especially as admission is free.

GINZA

Ginza, its name taken from the silver mint for a time located here during the Edo era, has long been synonymous with wealth. In the Meiji era, when the modernizing Meiji Government redeveloped parts of central Tokyo on European themes, it was Ginza that experienced perhaps the most major Western overhaul, wooden buildings and dirt streets gradually replaced by stone architecture and paved sidewalks, rickshaws by horse-drawn and eventually electric trams. Almost a hundred years before Ginza would become renowned for its high-end boutiques and bubble-era hostess clubs, where businessmen could comfortably drop hundreds of thousands of yen a night on expense account-funded hospitality, the area had already become one of Tokyo's most cosmopolitan and well-heeled districts.

Today, there are still some of those early Western-style buildings standing in Ginza. Now housing the prestigious Wako department store, the distinctive curved granite façade and clock tower of the Wako Building, on one corner of the Ginza Crossing, was first built in 1894 and then reconstructed after it was destroyed in the Great Kanto Earthquake of 1923. Across from it is the newer (relatively speaking, as it was built in 1930) but nonetheless venerable Mitsukoshi department store, the original branch of which is further down Chuo-dori in the Nihombashi district.

Mitsukoshi and Wako are two of many reasons Ginza has become so closely associated with high-end retail, both traditional and modern. Besides fashion, Chuo-dori is home to traditional stores such as paper and incense specialist Kyukyudo, which supplied the Imperial Palace with incense in the Edo era from its Kyoto store and eventually, in 1880, set up a branch in Ginza. Nearby are branches of Matsuya and Printemps department stores, while on and around Chuo-dori is a

ABOVE (INSET) A subway line entrance by the Ginza Crossing, with the historic Wako Building in the background.
ABOVE Jeweler Mikimoto's Ginza 2 Building, designed by 2013 Pritzker Prize-winning architect Toyo Ito, is one of Ginza's most distinctive structures.

OPPOSITE ABOVE LEFT Blvgari is one of many high-end fashion brands to have sleekly designed stores in Ginza.
OPPOSITE ABOVE RIGHT Another is Cartier, whose Tokyo flagship store is across from Bvlgari on Chuo-dori.
OPPOSITE BELOW Home to some of Tokyo's most exclusive restaurants, watering holes and places such as hostess clubs, Ginza is known just as much for its expensive nightlife as it is for its stores.

Who's Who of European fashion brands, from the up-market Burberry, Bvlgari, Cartier and Chanel to the more budget-friendly H&M and Zara.

Along with local brands like the jeweler Mikimoto and the affordable Muji and Uniqlo fashion chains, there is a strong contemporary architectural theme connecting Ginza's fashion brands. For scale alone, the Uniqlo flagship store, with 12 floors each covering 1,500 square meters is unprecedented for a single brand, while the Bvlgari Tower's attempt to look like a large jewelry box is almost as eye catching as the 10-story building opposite it that houses Chanel, its façade covered with 70,000 light-emitting diodes that paint changeable designs and patterns on the building's exterior. The silver mint may no longer be in Ginza, but a walk along Chuo-dori shows that Ginza is still very much minted.

Putting the icing on the cake is the food. Be it Italian, French or Japanese, Ginza is known for its fine dining, with amongst other things four of the 14 three-star Michelin restaurants in Tokyo located in the area. In particular, that includes some of Tokyo's most refined sushi restaurants, none more famous than Sukibayashi Jiro Honten, the three-star Michelin restaurant where octogenarian chef Jiro Ono has served a long list of celebrities and dignitaries that recently included a working dinner for Barack Obama and Japan's PM Shinzo Abe.

TSUKIJI MARKET AND KABUKI-ZA

Walking east from Ginza along Harumi-dori, the high-end brands are soon replaced by traditional elements of central Tokyo: Japan's premier venue for *kabuki*, its largest wholesale market and (covered separately in the next section) the historic Hamarikyu Garden, which began life as the duck hunting grounds of a Tokugawa shogun.

ABOVE Fresh cuts of tuna.
LEFT The market stalls at Tsukiji are open to the restaurant trade as well as the public.
RIGHT Super deep frozen tuna lined up for inspection before auction.

In the shape of the Kabuki-za Theater, it is the *kabuki*, a classical dance-drama featuring elaborate costumes and make-up and a very deliberate and stylized approach to both movement and speech, that comes first after leaving Ginza. There has been a theater on this site since the late 1880s, although the current classical looking theater is actually Kabuki-za's fifth incarnation. The first burned down in an electrical fire in 1921, the second was lost in the Great Kanto Earthquake of 1923, the third fell victim to Allied bombing in 1945, and the ageing fourth was pulled down in 2010 to make way for the current Kabuki-za, which reopened in 2013—a string of misfortunes that would make for a compelling *kabuki* play.

Further on from the theater comes the Tsukiji area, the name of which is indelibly linked with the Tokyo Metropolitan Central Wholesale market, simply known by most as Tsukiji Market or Tsukiji Fish Market, even though there is more than seafood here. Visit in the early hours of the morning and you will discover Tsukiji's fish auctions are as much of a performance art as the *kabuki*, only far more hectic and vocal, the slow choreography replaced by a blur of hand movements and signaling with which the city's finest sushi restaurants will drop millions of yen in an instance on a single tuna.

After that frenetic start, the multiple warehouses and inner and market areas that make up Tsukiji Market remain high octane all morning, with an estimated 60,000 wholesalers, buyers and shippers combining to trade 2,000 tons (or almost $20 million worth) of seafood and other fresh produce every day, something that would no doubt be unimaginable to Tsukiji's first fishermen, who were brought to the then mudflats of Tsukiji from Osaka in the late 1500s by Tokugawa Ieyasu to supply fish for his new power base.

TOP The Kabuki-za Theater before its latest renovation. The façade looks almost the same today, but there is now a gleaming skyscraper looming behind the theater.
CENTER LEFT The early morning tuna auctions.
LEFT One of the many seafood restaurants around Tsukiji Market. This one specializes in *donburi* (rice bowls) topped with fresh raw seafood such as salmon and salmon roe. Many others serve excellent fresh sushi from early morning till lunch.

HAMARIKYU GARDEN

In 1709, the sixth Tokugawa shogun, Ienobu, built a villa facing Tokyo Bay complete with sprawling gardens and duck ponds where he could indulge his passion for duck hunting. In the centuries since, Ienobu's hunting grounds have gone through various changes en route to becoming the garden visitors now see set against the towering modern skyscrapers of the Shiodome district.

The shogun's original wooden villa is no more, having burned down and then been rebuilt as a brick State guesthouse by the Meiji Foreign Ministry at the start of the Meiji era (1868–1912), for a short time thereafter being used to house visiting dignitaries such as former US president Grant and his wife when they came to Japan in 1879. In fact, Grant and the Emperor Meiji first met in a "floating" teahouse on one of the garden's ponds.

After World War II, ownership of the garden was transferred from the Imperial Household Agency to the Tokyo Metropolitan Government, who turned it into the current 24-hectare public park. Among the changes since then, the Nakajima-no-ochaya teahouse where Grant met the emperor has been rebuilt on the edge of Hamarikyu's main pond, its verandah overlooking waters which, unlike any other traditional garden pond in Tokyo, are tidal. The pines and cherry trees that accent the pond's edges give a very classic look, but the water that feeds the pond from Tokyo Bay fills it not with colorful ornamental carp but with eels, sea bass and black mullet.

In places, Hamarikyu is also a little more rugged than many traditional stroll gardens, especially so in the northern section of the garden where there are fields of peonies and canola alongside the more familiar plum grove feature. And no other garden in Tokyo, probably not in Japan, is served by water buses, which stop at Hamarikyu on routes that lead between Asakusa on the Sumida River and the man-made island of Odaiba in Tokyo Bay.

TOP One of the wooden bridges and walkways that lead visitors around and over Hamarikyu's ponds. ABOVE Rape blossoms are one of several seasonal blooms that transform parts of the garden each year.

ABOVE LEFT The garden's "floating" teahouse.
ABOVE Like many traditional gardens, Hamarikyu is designed to reflect seasonal changes. In autumn, red maples accentuate the green pines.
LEFT Spring cherry blossoms and the skyscrapers of Shiodome both illuminated at night.

EASTERN AND NORTHERN **TOKYO**

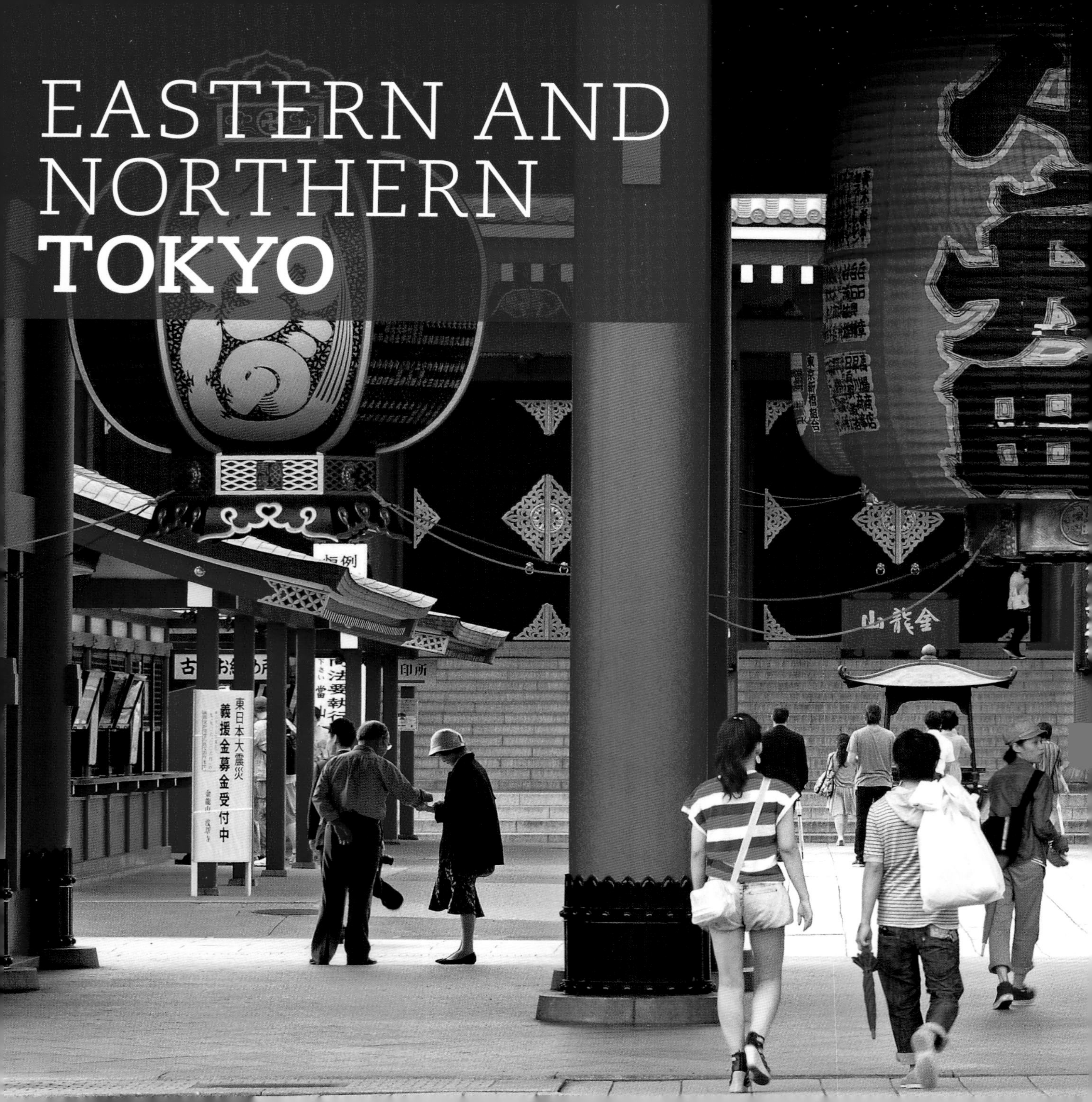

Yanaka Ginza
Nippori
SENDAGI
Asakura Sculpture Museum and Garden
YANAKA
Ogubashi-dori
Calligraphy Museum
NEGISHI
NIHONZUTSUMI
RYUSEN
Ichiyo Memorial Museum
KIYOKAWA
HASHIBA
YANAKA CEMETERY
UENO-SAKURAGI
SCAI the Bath House
Yoshida-ya Sake Shop Museum
Daimyo Tokei Clock Museum
MUKOGAOKA
SHITAYA
Showa-dori
IRIYA
SENZOKU
HIGASHI-ASAKUSA
HIGASHI-MUKOJIMA
IMADO
Heisei-kan
University Art Museum
Honkan Japanese Art Museum
TOKYO NATIONAL MUSEUM COMPLEX
Toyokan Asian Museum
National Museum of Nature and Science
National Museum of Western Art
Ueno Zoo
Tokyo Metropolitan Art Museum
Tosho-gu Shrine
UENO KOEN
Children's Zoo
Aquatic Zoo
Ueno Royal Museum
UENO STATION
Ueno District
NEZU
ATHLETIC FIELD
YAYOI
Yayoi Art Museum
TOKYO UNIVERSITY
KITA-UENO
MATSUGAYA
Kototoi-dori
Edo Shitamachi Traditional Crafts Museum
ASAKUSA
Hanayashiki Amusement Park
Senso-ji Temple
SUMIDA PARK
Sumida City Museum
Amuse Museum
Main Hall
Five Storey Pagoda
Hozomon Gate
Rokku Broadway
HANAKAWADO
MUKOJIMA
HIGASHI-UENO
NISHI-ASAKUSA
Kappabashi-dori
Hongan-ji
Taiko Drum Museum
Nakamise-dori Shopping Street
Kaminari-mon (Thunder Gate)
Asakusa
Asahi Beer Hall
Tokyo Sky Tree
Oshiage
Tokyo Skytree
IKENOHATA
Shinobazu Pond
Kyu Iwasaki-tei House & Gardens
Shitamachi History Museum
Ameya Yokocho Street Market
Inaricho
Tawaramachi
KAMINARI-MON
MOTO-ASAKUSA
AZUMABASHI
Honjo-azumabashi
Bunkyo Museum
Tokyo Univ. Museum
Kasuga
Korakuen
Hongo-sanchome
Ueno-okachimachi
Shin-okachimachi
KOTOBUKI
Ace World Bag & Luggage Museum
KOMAGATA
NIRIHIRA
LaQua
Big O Ferris Wheel
Baseball Hall of Fame
UENO
Kasuga-dori
Kuramae
HIGASHI-KOMAGATA
YOKOKAWA
Tokyo Dome City
Tokyo Waterworks History Museum
Japan Football Museum
Origami Kaikan
KOJIMA
MISUJI
TAITO
KURAMAE
HONJO
Suidobashi
Tokyo Wonder Site Hongo
Kanda Myojin
Tokyo Anime Center Akiba
Torigoe
Kuramae-bashi-dori
ISHIWARA
TAIHEI
Sumida River
Shuro Expressway No.7 Mukojima Line
Shuro E'way No.1 Ueno Line
MISAKICHO
SARUGAKUCHO
Ochanomizu
SOTO-KANDA
Akihabara
Yodobashi Akiba
ASAKUSA BASHI
EARTHQUAKE MEMORIAL PARK
Kuramaebashi-dori
NISHI-KANDA
KANDA-SURUGADAI
Meiji Univ. Museum Archaeology & Criminal Materials Exhibition
Nikolai Cathedral
Old Transportation Museum
KANDA-SAKUMACHO
YANAGIBASHI
Docomo History
KINSHI
KANDA-JIMBOCHO
KANDA-SUDACHO
Asakusabashi
YOKOAMI
Ryogoku
KAMEZAWA
Jimbocho
KANDA-OGAWAMACHI
HIGASHI-KANDA
Sumo Stadium, Sumo Museum
Edo-Tokyo Museum
Sobu Line
Kinshicho
Iwamotocho
IWAMOTOCHO
NIHOMBASHI-BAKUROCHO
RYOGOKU
Keiyo-doro
Keiyo-dori
HIGASHI-NIHOMBASHI
MIDORI
KOTOBASHI
Science Museum
HITOTSUBASHI
KANDA-NISHIKICHO
Kanda
Bakurocho
Kiri-no-Museum
Shuro Expressway No.7 Komatsugawa Line
CHITOSE
TATEKAWA
MORI
National Museum of Modern Art
Takebashi
Kodenmacho
Shin-nihombashi
KIKUKAWA
HAMACHO PARK
Hamacho
SHIN-OHASHI
Shin-ohashi-dori
Morishita
Kikukawa
SUMIYOSHI
The Imperial Palace East Garden
NINO-MARU AREA
Museum of Imperial Collections
Communications Museum
Mitsui Memorial Museum
Ningyocho
NIHOMBASHI-NINGYOCHO
NIHOMBASHI HAMACHO
HON-MARU AREA
Otemachi
Currency Museum
Hanzomon Line
MORISHITA
SARUE
Visitor Center
IMPERIAL PALACE GROUNDS
Mitsukoshimae
TOKIWA
Kite Museum
Nihombashi
Kiyosumi-shirakawa
Kiyosubashi-dori
TOKYO STATION
Suitengumae
KIYOSUMI
SHIRAKAWA
THE IMPERIAL PALACE OUTER GARDEN
Kayabacho
NIHOMBASHI KAKIGARACHO
KIYOSUMI PARK
Fukagawa Edo Folk Museum
MIYOSHI
Museum of Contemporary Art Tokyo
Mitsubishi Ichigokan Museum
Bridgestone Museum of Art
KAYABACHO
Marunouchi My Plaza
Idemitsu Museum of Arts
Kiyosumi Gardens
FUKUZUMI
HIRANO
Shuto E'way No.9 Fukagawa Line
KIBA PARK
Imperial Theatre
Tokyo Int'l Forum
Yurakucho
KYOBASHI
HATCHOBORI
SHINKAWA
SAGA
Police Museum
National Film Center
FUKAGAWA
Kasaibashi-dori
Hibiya Park
YURAKUCHO
Hibiya
Ginza-Itchome
Hatchobori
EITAI
MONZEN-NAKACHO
Kasumigaseki
500 m
1000 feet
scale 1 : 30 000
N

TOKYO'S EASTERN AND NORTHERN DISTRICTS

During the Edo era, the low-lying areas east of what is now the Imperial Palace (then it was the site of Edo Castle) developed under the strict social hierarchy of Tokugawa rule into the home of artisans, merchants and laborers, at that time considered the lowest rungs on Japan's social ladder. In this *shitamachi* (literally the "low city" in reference to the level of the land), a rich working-class culture grew, and today it is in these neighborhoods where old Edo is at its most visible within modern Tokyo.

It is the *shitamachi* that has perhaps more than anything defined the Tokyoite. While the samurai of the "high city" were preserving traditions and were confined by rigid social rank, it was the residents of the *shitamachi* who drove Edo and then Tokyo forward, developing once "lower" arts like *ukiyo-e* and *kabuki*, creating Tokyo's great festivals (all held east of the palace), and driving entrepreneurism and innovation to better their lot. The lines are blurred somewhat today, but it is still in neighborhoods like Asakusa and Ueno that the *shitamachi* heart beats the loudest.

AKIHABARA

Situated just to the northeast of the Imperial Palace area, Akihabara is where central Tokyo begins to transition into the traditional "low city", not that you would know it if you only visited Chuo-dori, the main street running through Akihabara, and the home electronics stores that now congregate there.

Those stores, which have given Akihabara the tag of being Tokyo's "home electronics capital", can trace their roots to the immediate aftermath of World War II when the black market trading of radio and electrical components took off in the area, eventually developing through Japan's recovery and surge in technological expertise into a legitimate focal point for the latest technology and home electronics. Walk around Akihabara today and alongside small back-street electrical parts stores and used computer shops, such as the several branches of Sofmap, you will see high-tech stores specializing in things like robotics as well as home electronic megastores like Akky, Ishimaru Denki, Laox and the giant Yodobashi Akiba that dominates Akihabara Station's east side.

Whether Akihabara still offers the great duty free deals that made it a major stop on the tourist trail is up for debate. The latest tech? Yes. The best prices? Maybe not. But there is another more recent side to Akihabara that guarantees it will have international recognition for some time to come: *otaku*.

On the back of video gaming in the late 1980s, but more recently through *anime* (animation) and *manga* (comics), Akihabara has become ground zero for Japanese and latterly international *otaku* (geeks). It was Akihabara (or Akiba as it is often called) that gave birth to the maid café, where young waitresses typically dressed in French maid outfits and affecting extreme cuteness fawn over stereotypically socially awkward *otaku* customers. And it is in Akihabara where you will find Tokyo's biggest and best *anime* and *manga* stores in the shape of places such as Animate and Mandrake, as well as stores like Donkihote and Gee Store Akiba that sell cosplay outfits and the like, video game stores, such as the classics-filled Retro Game Camp and the new game-focused Trader, not to mention places specializing in model kits, *anime* character goods, and a range of retro and high-tech "game centers" (video arcades). It is no surprise that Akihabara is said to be the center point of a global *otaku* consumer market now worth more than 400 billion yen annually.

For a very stark contrast to the electronics and *otaku*, you only need walk several hundred meters west of Chuo-dori to one of Tokyo's most important shrines, Kanda Myojin. Established in the 730s near what was once the site of Edo Castle, now the Imperial Palace area, shogun Tokugawa Ieyasu moved the shrine to its current location in 1616, supposedly in an effort to distance his castle, and rule, from the rebellious influence of Taira-no-Masakado, an anti-authority figure from the 900s, who was enshrined in Kanda Myojin and whose popularity was still high with Edo's population.

While Masakado no longer has such an effect on Tokyoites, Kanda Matsuri, the shrine's centuries-old festival, has given Kanda Myojin a special place in modern Tokyo. Held annually on the weekend closest to May 15, although only on a grand scale in years ending in odd numbers, the *matsuri* features processions of men in Edo-era costumes, portable shrine carriers and priests on horseback, quite a striking sight as they pass through the modern city.

LEFT Beside the home electronics megastores, Akihabara has a thriving second-hand scene for everything from used PCs and video games to hobby collectibles. The duty free stores might not offer the greatest bargains any more, but if you are happy rummaging through boxes and packed shelves in tiny back-street stores, you will be able to pick up great deals on used items that tend to be in excellent condition.

FAR LEFT Akihabara is a great place to buy the latest console and PC games.
LEFT Chuo-dori, the main street of Akihabara.

ABOVE The entrance to the Kanda Myojin Shrine, a short walk east of Akihabara and the focal point of one of Tokyo's most impressive annual festivals, the Kanda Matsuri.
RIGHT A twist on the typical Akihabara maid café theme. Instead of young waitresses fawning over male *otaku*, this place has a young female clientele served by men in maid outfits.

ASAKUSA AND SENSO-JI

Asakusa, situated alongside the Sumida River in the heart of Tokyo's *shitamachi*, has played a prominent role in the history and development of Tokyo ever since Senso-ji Temple was established here in the 620s. As with many ancient Japanese stories, there is an overlapping of fact and fiction at play in the tale of how Senso-ji was born, legend having it that the temple was created to enshrine a golden image of Kannon, the goddess of mercy, supposedly caught in the nets of two local brothers as they fished the Sumida-gawa. Even though the brothers at first tried to throw the statue away, the more mythical part of the tale goes that it kept returning to their nets.

Some 1,400 years on and the current incarnation of the Senso-ji Temple complex is one of Tokyo's most striking sights, greeting visitors with a 12-meter high, 12-meter wide roofed gateway called the Kaminari-mon (Thunder Gate), on either side of which are the fierce-looking bronze guardian statues of Raijin and Fujin (the gods of thunder and wind). Rounding out the spectacle, a 680-kilogram red paper lantern hangs underneath the gateway, almost always in a sea of tourists posing for photos beside it.

Some people will point to the colorful stalls immediately beyond Kaminari-mon, on Nakamise-dori, that sell, alongside fine traditional crafts, snacks and clothing, cheap and cheerful tourist trinkets and T-shirts and say that Senso-ji has become too touristy. Maybe so, but the complex is still a tremendous sight, of which the Kaminari-mon is just the tip of the iceberg.

At the other end of Nakamise-dori stands the two-story, 22-meter-high Hozomon Gate, decorated with three giant lanterns and two 362-kilogram straw sandals. In answer to the Kaminari-mon's Raijin and Fujin, the precious relics stored on the upper level of the Hozomon are protected by two menacing 5-meter-tall statues of Nio, the guardian deity of the Buddha, who command a view toward Senso-ji's five-story pagoda and imposing main hall.

TOP Senso-ji's pagoda and Hozomon Gate. Rebuilt after being destroyed in air raids in March 1945, the current gateway employs modern disaster-prevention equipment to protect the treasures now stored in its upper levels. **ABOVE** Visitors waft incense smoke over themselves in front of Senso-ji's main hall. The pungent smoke is said to have curative effects for all manner of ailments.

Leaving Senso-ji behind, there is more to Asakusa than its temple. For a hundred years leading up to World War II, the area was Tokyo's main entertainment district, and an important part of that, Rokku Broadway, is still home to theaters like Engei Hall, where the daily bill includes a variety of traditional *shitamachi*-born forms of comedy and story-telling. *Rakugo* performances, in which a seated comic weaves long, complicated comic tales, and *manzai*, where a comic duo comprised of a straight man (*tsukommi*) and funny man (*boke*) bounce one-liners and quips off of each other at breakneck speed, are the most common acts on show.

Hanayashiki, Japan's oldest amusement park, slightly north of Rokku Broadway, is another remnant. Originally opened in 1853 as a flower garden and then housing a zoo for some years, it became an amusement park proper shortly after World War II and developed into one of Tokyo's premier entertainment venues—the Disney or Universal Studios Japan of its time. The roller coaster here is not only the oldest in Japan, having debuted in 1953, but quite possibly the least terrifying, only reaching 40 kilometers per hour as it clunks over and around the rest of the tiny Hanayashiki's retro attractions, at times providing unblurred views across Senso-ji to Tokyo Skytree.

But perhaps at no time does Asakusa's history come to life as much as it does in May during the centuries-old Sanja Matsuri, a festival held in honor of Senso-ji's founders. Some two million onlookers take to the streets of Asakusa, centered around Senso-ji, to watch frenetic processions of portable shrines (*mikoshi*) that are bounced through the heaving streets by teams of sweat-drenched (and sometimes saké-fueled) pall bearers.

ABOVE Crowds typical of a weekend visit to Senso-ji passing under the Hozomon's three giant lanterns.

TOP Fortune card drawers at Senso-ji. You select your drawer by age (the uppermost drawer in this photo is for 16 year olds, the lower for 17 year olds) and then pick out a piece of paper with your fortune on it. If it is good, keep it. If not, tying the paper to the rack near the fortune boxes is said to dispel any misfortune.
ABOVE Fans for sale on Nakamise-dori. In this case, the designs are very much aimed at tourists.
RIGHT Nakamise-dori in a rare quiet moment. While many of the stores here specialize in touristy goods, the vibrant street is also a great place to pick up traditional sweets and snacks as well as items such as casual cotton *yukata* gowns.

From near and far, the 634-meter Tokyo Skytree has come to dominate Tokyo's eastern skyline.

TOKYO SKYTREE AND ASAHI BEER HALL

East of Asakusa, across the gently rippled waters of the Sumida River, Tokyo's newest landmark combines with one of the city's oddest modern architectural sights to create what is arguably now east Tokyo's most distinctive view. At 634 meters, the white metallic lattice frame of Tokyo Skytree, the new landmark in question, rises above Tokyo's east side like a glistening spear thrust to the heavens, punctuating the skyline and visible from all parts of the city even before its completion in 2012.

Built over four years by Tobu Railway and a group of six terrestrial broadcasters for the dual purpose of being a radio/television broadcast tower and forming the centerpiece of a multi-building commercial development that also comprises restaurants, office spaces and amusement facilities, Skytree has become one of Tokyo's biggest tourist attractions. In Skytree's first week of business, some 1.6 million people visited the tower. In the first year, the figure topped 50 million.

The main reasons for that popularity, besides the insatiable Japanese thirst for anything new, are the height and the views. Ranked

BELOW At the base of Tokyo Skytree.
BOTTOM The view from Asakusa on the other side of the Sumida River. Tokyo Skytree stands alongside the offices of Asahi Breweries. The golden flame on top of the smaller of the Asahi buildings is one of Tokyo's most recognizable architectural sights and has brought the building a memorable, if not unfortunate, nickname. Thanks to the shape of the "flame", locals call it *unchi biru* (turd building).

behind the 829.9-meter Burj Khalifa in Dubai, Skytree is the second tallest structure in the world, and from its observations decks, one 450 meters up, the other a still vertigo-inducing 350 meters, the 360-degree views of Tokyo and beyond are simply breathtaking.

But what about the odd-looking building that shares the Sumida River skyline with Skytree? We have architect Philippe Starck and the company he designed it for, Asahi Beer, to thank for that. Completed in 1989, the building serves as Asahi's head office, and design-wise certainly appears to pay homage to Asahi's products. Beside a stout building with a polished black granite façade on top of which sits a 300-ton golden "flame", stands a taller building, with a shimmering golden exterior and foam-shaped white roof designed to look like a glass of chilled lager.

By day, Skytree and Starck's creation together form a startling sight, a near-hypnotic eyesore. Illuminated at night, when both seem to hover above the Sumida River, which itself is accented by the orange lanterns of the *yakatabune* (houseboats-turned-floating restaurants) plying the water, it is just mesmerizing.

THE SUMIDA RIVER

On the last Saturday of July every year, the evening skies above the Sumida River explode into life with the Sumidagawa Hanabi Taikai. During the annual fireworks display, 20,000 rockets paint a kaleidoscope of colors over eastern Tokyo, attracting hundreds of thousands of onlookers to Asakusa, Ryogoku and other neighborhoods on the banks of the Sumida-gawa.

The Sumida fireworks festival can be traced back to 1732, when it started as part of the summer *o-bon* (festival of the dead) celebrations, and under the name Ryogoku Kawabiraki cemented itself as a popular annual event, a rare opportunity for the poverty-stricken masses living in the *shitamachi* areas through which the Sumida River passes to enjoy an evening of celebration. After a hiatus from World War II until the late 1970s, the festival once again became one of Tokyo's biggest and most vibrant annual events, not just with the fireworks themselves but also with the street food stalls, the colorful cotton *yukata* worn by many in attendance and the heaving crowds that are a part of every Japanese summer festival.

If a visit to the Sumida River for the fireworks allows you to experience a centuries-old celebration, a trip down the river any time of year affords a glimpse of both Tokyo's past and its present. Tokyo's broad network of waterways, at the centre of which is the Sumida-gawa, were the commercial arteries through which flowed the lifeblood of Tokyo's development. Take a trip down the river on one of the water buses that run between Asakusa, Hamarikyu Gardens, Odaiba and other parts of the bay area, and you will still see giant barges carrying industrial material, joined after nightfall by the orange lanterns of the *yakatabune* houseboats that today serve as floating *izakaya*.

With Skytree fading, although never quite disappearing, as the boats head south toward Tokyo Bay, the varied faces of the city unfold beside the river. You will see industrial units churning out smog and luxury high-rise apartment blocks, *futon* hanging on the balconies of lower-rise homes and people cycling and jogging along the banks, anglers fishing the murky waters alongside the cardboard homes of the homeless covered by blue tarpaulin to keep out the rain. Not quite the Olympic 2020 PR images of Tokyo, or the usual guidebook shots of cosplayers in Harajuku, but views of the city that are much more familiar to most Tokyoites.

OPPOSITE ABOVE A futuristic looking riverboat docked at Asakusa on the Sumida River. **ABOVE** The same boat runs down the Sumida as far as Rainbow Bridge and the Odaiba area, providing great views and insights into Tokyo life.

FAR LEFT Tokyo Skytree and the annual Sumida River fireworks display combine to illuminate the night skies of eastern Tokyo. The banks of the Sumida-gawa are crowded for the late July event, with many people staking down their spots days in advance.
LEFT The Sumida passing under the Kachidoki Bridge in Chuo Ward. In all, the Sumida-gawa passes through seven of Tokyo's 23 wards after it branches off from the Arakawa River, the result of a Meiji-era anti-flooding diversion, the other six wards being Kita, Adachi, Arakawa, Sumida, Taito and Koto.

UENO

In many respects, Ueno, like Asakusa, is still firmly connected to its *shitamachi* roots. In others, it has become more eclectic. Ueno's Ameya Yokocho street market, which begins just across the road from Ueno Station's main exit and then runs south along a narrow street next to elevated train lines, is *shitamachi* to the core, and like the electronics in Akihabara flourished on the back of black market trading as Tokyo rebuilt and then boomed after World War II. The difference with the bustling Ameyoko, as it is familiarly known, is that instead of home electronics, the focus of the small stalls here is a mix of fresh fish and vegetables, herbal medicines and teas and low-price clothing and bags.

Nearby Ueno Koen is a very different affair. The park has the greatest concentration of top-class museums in Tokyo, with the Shitamachi History Museum, Tokyo Metropolitan Art Museum, National Museum of Nature and Science, University Art Museum, National Museum of Western Art and Tokyo National Museum all in or skirting its edge. The Tokyo National Museum, in particular, is an incredible facility, housing some 100,000 artifacts that date from 3000 BC (during the Jomon period) to the late 19th century and covering everything from Japanese sculpture, woodblock prints, calligraphy and ceramics to a special collection of 300 7th- and 8th-century priceless treasures from Horyu-ji Temple in Nara. At the other side of Ueno Park, the Shitamachi History Museum offers a different insight into Japan's past, with a focus on the history of Tokyo's *shitamachi*, of which Ueno is an integral part. From the outside, the gray building is about as drab as museums come, but the exhibits inside, especially the reconstruction of a 1920s *shitamachi* tenement row, give a real sense of how life once was in this part of Tokyo.

Away from the museums, Ueno Park's 54 hectacres of grounds are also home to Tokyo's biggest zoo and a Tosho-gu shrine, which like the Tosho-gu in Nikko (page 114) was built in the 1600s for shogun Tokugawa Ieyasu and also shares a similar five-story pagoda, while the park's lily-covered Shinobazu Pond is a focal point for food vendors at weekends. The best time to see the park, however, is spring. In late March and early April, the fleeting pink blossom of the park's cherry trees makes Ueno one of the most popular spots for *hanami* (cherry blossom viewing) parties in Tokyo, which in true *shitamachi* fashion tend to be mass saké-fueled picnics rather than a quiet contemplation of the ephemeralness of nature.

ABOVE All that remains of the Ueno Daibutsu (Great Buddha), which once stood in what is now Ueno Park. Built in the 1630s, the seated statue was damaged by fire and earthquakes before finally being toppled by the Great Kanto Earthquake of 1923 and eventually melted down during WW II. **LEFT** When the annual wave of cherry blossom hits Tokyo in spring, Ueno Park is one of the most popular places for *hanami* (cherry blossom viewing parties).

OPPOSITE ABOVE Shinobazu Pond in Ueno Park.
OPPOSITE BELOW The bustling Ameya Yokocho street market.
RIGHT The Gallery of Horyu-ji Treasures at the Tokyo National Museum.

ABOVE Street food vendors are a common sight in Ueno Park, especially around the Shinobazu Pond area, where it is possible to come across such items as savory *okonomiyaki* pancakes (pictured), *yakitori* (grilled chicken skewers) and traditional sweet treats.

KIYOSUMI GARDEN

For a city with a reputation in some quarters for being a mostly unattractive, gray slab of urban sprawl, occasionally punctuated by architecturally striking high-rises, in others seemingly crumbling away in anticipation of bulldozers and the next redevelopment, Tokyo has a surprising richness of green spaces and, in particular, traditional gardens. Among them all, Kiyosumi Teien has few equals.

Although dating to the Edo era, when it was part of the residence of a well-known business magnate called Kinokuniya Bunzaemon (1669–1733) and then later the Edo home of the lord of Sekiyado Castle in Chiba, the garden's current shape was not created until the Meiji era when the grounds came into the hands of Iwasaki Yataro, the founder of Mitsubishi, in 1878. Iwasaki created the traditional garden visitors see now as a place of relaxation for his employees (an idea modern-day companies are now retaking to in Tokyo with rooftop greenery) and to entertain visiting dignitaries.

Kiyosumi's most striking feature after the garden's two-year Iwasaki-funded makeover, is its central pond, punctuated by three islands on which herons can often be seen perched on ornamental pines. Encircling the water, pathways lead visitors through a succession of views, from an artificial azalea-covered hill modeled on Mount Fuji, which blooms into life in May, through to a small iris garden and a *sukiya*-style teahouse that juts out over the pond, casting a shimmering reflection as it does so.

ABOVE You will see hints of the city in the background, but otherwise Kiyosumi manages to feel removed from modern-day Tokyo. The garden also benefits from a fairly unfashionable location in eastern Tokyo's Koto ward, which has kept it off the usual tourist trail and for the most part free of crowds. On some weekdays, you can almost feel like you have a corner of the garden to yourself.

Alongside the water features, stones also play a prominent role in Kiyosumi's landscaping, and none more so that the *iso-watari* stepping stone pathways that lead across shallow parts of the pond, taking visitors closer to the colorful carp and turtles that call the water home. Some of the other stone features, however, are easy to overlook. The Basho Stone, on which is carved Matsuo Basho's famous haiku, "Furu ike ya, kawazu tobikomu, mizu no oto" (translated best by noted haiku translator R. H. Blyth as "The old pond, a frog jumps in, the sound of water"), is tucked away in a corner near a lovely side garden that blooms with irises in June, while the collection of large stones brought by the Iwasaki family from across Japan and positioned around the garden, could easily be missed if you cannot read the Japanese on the wooden name markers next to them.

ABOVE Like so many traditional Japanese gardens, Kiyosumi transforms with each season. In autumn, the garden is given a richness as its trees take on reds and yellows that eventually fall and accent the walkways. In summer, everything is a lush green and the pond dazzles in the high sun.

LEFT The occasional sound of gently trickling water is a feature of many traditional gardens.

ABOVE AND LEFT The large stepping stones and slabs that skirt Kiyosumi's pond are one of the garden's defining features.

SOUTHERN TOKYO

Oedo Line
Banknote & Postage Stamp Museum
Jimbocho
Kudanshita
Yasukuni Shrine
Showakan
Ogawamachi
Iwamotocho
HIGASHI-KANDA
SHINJUKU
Akebonobashi
SHINJUKU STATION
KUDAN-MINAMI
Science Museum
Shinjuku Line
Ichigaya
KITA-NO-MARU PARK
Chidorigafuchi Water Park
Craft Gallery
Takebashi
Mita Line
Chiyoda Line
Awajicho
Kanda
KANDA-NISHIKICHO
UCHI-KANDA
IWAMOTOCHO
Hibiya Line
Bakurocho
Bakuro Yokohama
Koden-macho
Higashi-nihombashi
HIGASHI-NIHOM
Shin-nihombashi
Sobu Line
Hamacho
Shinjuku-sanchome
Tokyo Toy Museum
Nanboku Line
Yurakucho Line
Hanzomon Line
KOKYO
Museum of Imperial Collections
THE IMPERIAL PALACE EAST GARDEN
OTEMACHI
Communications Museum
Ningyocho
Shinjuku-gyoenmae
Yotsuya-sanchome
Marunouchi Line
JCII Camera Museum
IMPERIAL PALACE GROUNDS
Imperial Palace
Wadakura Fountain Park
NIHOMBASHI HAMACHO
Suiten-gu Shrine
SHINJUKU GYOEN NATIONAL GARDEN
Yotsuya
WAKABA
KOJIMACHI
HIRAKAWACHO
SHIMIZUDANI PARK
Nijubashi-mae
MARUNOUCHI
TOKYO STATION
YAESU
NIHOMBASHI
Nihombashi
Suitengumae
KAYABACHO
Minami-shinjuku
Yoyogi
Sendagaya
Kokuritsu-kyogijo
Shinanomachi
Chuo Line
Oedo Line
Nijubashi Bridge
THE IMPERIAL PALACE OUTER GARDEN
Hanzomon Line
Kayabacho
Tokyo Int'l Forum
Imperial Theater
Tozai Line
Meiji Shrine
SENDAGAYA
Kitasando
AKASAKA DETACHED PALACE GARDEN
Akasaka-mitsuke
Sakuradamon
KASUMIGASEKI PARK
KYOBASHI
SAGA
MOTO-AKASAKA
NAGATACHO
Hibiya-dori
Takaracho
SHINKAWA
MEIJI OUTER GARDEN
Oedo Line
National Diet Bldg Kokkai Gijido
Marunouchi Line
Hibiya Park
Hibiya
Yurakucho
Tokyo E'way
Hatchobori
Tokyo (Keiyo Line)
Aoyama-itchome
HATCHOBORI
YOYOGI PARK
HARAJUKU
Kasumigaseki
Ginza-itchome
SHINTOMI
IRIFUNE
EITAI
Tameike-sanno
Chiyoda Line
Akasaka
Ginza Line
Ginza
GINZA
Shintomicho
Ota Memorial Museum of Ukiyo-e Art
Hanzomon Line & Ginza Line
Gaiemmae
NOGI PARK
21_21 Design Sight Museum
Okura Museum
Toranomon
Uchisaiwaicho
Yamanote Line
Ginza Noh Theater
Higashi-ginza
Kabuki-za Theater
MINATO
TSUKUDA-KOEN PARK
Harajuku
JINGUMAE
MIDTOWN GARDEN
Roppongi-itchome
NISHI-SHIMBASHI
Panasonic Shiodome Museum
Tsukiji
Hibiya Line
TSUKUDA
TSUKISHIMA ISLAND
Etchujima
Meiji-jingumae
KITA-AOYAMA
MINAMI-AOYAMA
AOYAMA CEMETERY
Nogizaka
Suntory Museum of Art
TOKYO MIDTOWN
TORANOMON
Sakurada-dori
Shimbashi
Shimbashi Embujo Theater
JINAN
Omotesando-dori
Fukutoshin Line
Omotesando
OMOTESANDO
National Art Center
ROPPONGI
Laforet Museum
ATAGO
ATAGO HILLS
NHK Broadcast Museum
Toei Mita Line
Shio Sight
Shiodome
Tsukiji-shijo
TSUKIJI
Tsukishima
Sumidagawa River
ETCHU
Tobacco & Salt Museum
Chiyoda Line
AOYAMA PARK
Roppongi
Hibiya Line
AZABUDAI
Kamiyacho
ATAGO GREEN HILLS
Onarimon
TSUKISHIMA
SHIBUYA
Aoyama-dori
Nezu Museum
Okamoto Taro Memorial Museum
Mori Art Museum
ROPPONGI HILLS
SHIBA-KOEN
Hamarikyu Garden
Tsukiji Central Wholesale Market
Oedo Line
Kachidoki
SHIN-TSUKISHIMA PARK
Yurakucho Line
SHIBUYA STATION
Roppongi-dori
Striped House Museum of Museum
Tokyo Tower
Zojo-ji Temple
Daibonsho
Sangedatsu-mon
Daiden
Kyozo
KidZania
Tokyu Toyoko Line
Shibuya Ward Museum
Azabujuban
HIGASHI-AZABU
SHIBA PARK
Daimon
SHIBA DETACHED PALACE GARDENS
KACHIDOKI
HARUMI
Urban Dock Lalaport Toyosu
TOYOS
HIGASHI
HIRO-O
Yamatane Museum of Art
Hibiya Line
MOTO-AZABU
Akabanebashi
AZABU-JUBAN
SHIBA-DAIMON
Shibakoen
Hamamatsucho
Takeshiba
Hiro-o
PRINCE ARISUGAWA MEMORIAL PARK
SHIBA
Sakurada-dori
Daikanyama
Ebisu
MINAMI-AZABU
MITA
Mita
Hinode
EBISU-NISHI
Nanboku Line
Meguro Line
EBISU
Shuto E'way No.2 Meguro Line
KAIGAN
Shijomae
Shin-toyosu
Naka-meguro
Nakameguro
Yebisu Beer Museum
Tamachi
Toei Asakusa Line
Tokyo Monorail
Yurikamome Line
Shibaura-futo
N
Tokyo Bay
SHIROKANE
Shirokane-tanakawa
SHIBAURA
Tokyo Metro Museum of Photography
Yebisu Garden
NAKA MEGURO PARK
Matsuoka Museum of Art
MITA
Saikyo Line
Yamanote Line
SHIROKANEDAI
Namboku & Mita
Shirokanedai
Institute for Nature Study
HAPPO-EN GARDEN
Sengaku-ji
Sengakuji
Shibau
1 km
1 mile
scale 1 : 45 000
Ariake Tennis-no-mori
Ariake Coliseum
NAKA-MEGURO
Tokyo Metro Teien Art Museum
Kume Art Museum
Meguro Museum of Art
TAKANAWA
Yurikamome Line
Rainbow Bridge
Ariake Tennis-no-mori Park
Meguro
MEGURO
Hatakeyama Kinenkan Museum
KAMI-OSAKI
Takanawadai
Asakusa Line
Dai-ichi Keihin
DAI-ROKU DAIBA
DAI-SAN DAIBA HISTORICAL PARK
ODAIBA BEACH PARK
Shuto Expressway Wan
Kokusai-tenjijo
Wanza Ariake
ARIAKE
Meguro Parasitologi
Sugino Costume Museum
HIGASHI-GOTANDA
Shinagawa
Takanawa-mon
Museum of Fishery Sciences
Shuto Expressway No.1 Haneda Line
Decks Tokyo Beach, Madamme Tussauds
DAIBA
Odaibakaihinkoen
Water Science Museum
SHIMO-MEGURO
EPSON Aqua Stadium
KONAN PARK
Aqua City
Joyopolis
Tokyoteleport
Meguro Fudo Temple
NISHI-GOTANDA
Gotanda
Sony Historical Museum
KONAN
Daiba
Ferris Weel
Rinkai-shinkotsu Line
Fudomae
Tokyu Meguro Line
Daini Keihin
Rinkai Line
Rinkai Line
Odaiba
Aomi
KOYAMADAI
Tokyu Ikegami Line
Osaki-hirokoji
Hara Museum of Contemporary Art
Kita-shinagawa
SHIOKAZE PARK
Fune-no-kagakukan
FERRY FUTO PARK
Musashikoyama
Tennoz u-Isle
Shinagawa Keihin Keikyo Line
AOMI
National Museum of Emerging Science and Innovation
KOYAMA
O Art Museum
Museum of Maritime Science
KITA-SHINAGAWA
Osaki
Tokyo-ko Tunnel
Telecomcenter
Toei Asakusa Line
Togoshi-ginza
Yokosuka Line & Tokaido Shinkansen
Nishi-Koyama
EBARA
OSAKI
TOGOSHI
Shin-Baba
HIGASHI-SHINAGAWA
YASHIO
Odaiba Hot Spring Theme Park

TOKYO'S SOUTHERN DISTRICTS

Moving away from the very center of Tokyo, heading southwest, Roppongi is a prime example of how new and old in Tokyo manage to coexist with apparently very little friction. On the one hand, there are cosmopolitan urban complexes like Roppongi Hills and Tokyo Midtown, on the other hand, a sight like Zojo-ji, which under Tokugawa patronage in the Edo era became one of Japan's most important Buddhist temples. Head southeast and the contrasts are just as visible. As well as the fashionable Ebisu, Meguro and Daikanyama neighborhoods is Shinagawa and the temple at the center of the historic tale of the 47 Ronin, while out in Tokyo Bay, the man-made island of Odaiba, once part of Edo-era canon batteries, has been given a modern makeover to become Tokyo's most entertaining family day out.

ROPPONGI

Nowhere else in Tokyo has undergone the kind of transformation that Roppongi has seen since the early 2000s. What used to be a late night destination for drinkers, clubbers and restaurant-goers, but by day was a fairly unspectacular slice of urbanity, has since become one of Tokyo's most cosmopolitan neighborhoods.

RIGHT Before and since the arrival of the Roppongi Hills and Tokyo Midtown urban redevelopments, Roppongi has had a reputation for its nightlife, with an incredible range of bars, clubs and restaurants, from fashionable nightclubs to Michelin-starred Japanese dining.

The catalyst for Roppongi's makeover was construction tycoon Minoru Mori's decision to use Roppongi as the site for the multi-billion dollar Roppongi Hills complex, which was opened, dubbed "a city within a city", in 2003. It is not hard to see why it got that moniker. Centered around a 54-story tower atop of which is one of Tokyo's leading contemporary art galleries, the Mori Art Museum, the complex incorporates office spaces, luxury apartments, shops, restaurants, cafés, a multi-screen movie theater, a five-star hotel, an outdoor amphitheater and the headquarters of one of Japan's major television networks, Asahi TV.

Four years later, when Roppongi Hills got a neighbor and rival in the shape of another "city within a city",

LEFT Tokyo City View, the observation deck atop the Mori Tower at Roppongi Hills.

BELOW: Louise Bourgeois's spider sculpture "Maman" stands guard at Roppongi Hills. The sculpture has become a Roppongi landmark, greeting visitors to Roppongi Hills as they step off the giant escalator that leads from Roppongi subway station.

BELOW The Arena at Roppongi Hills is the venue for a variety of events and live performances.

BELOW One of the features of Tokyo Midtown is the art. Besides being home to venues such as 21_21 Design Sight, FujiFilm Square and the Suntory Museum of Art, there are sculptures and other art works from globally recognized artists scattered around the grounds.

ABOVE The National Art Center. **LEFT** The 21_21 Design Sight gallery and workshop within the grounds of Tokyo Midtown. It is because of major venues like these, as well as many other smaller galleries and the annual Roppongi Art Night, that Roppongi has become known as something of an artistic center. Looking at the design of these facilities, not to mention places like Hills and Midtown, and it is clear why Roppongi is also famed for its architecture.

Roppongi's transformation was all but complete. Like Roppongi Hills, the five buildings that comprise Tokyo Midtown include a giant central tower, at 248 meters the tallest building in Tokyo Prefecture, and a sleek mix of restaurants, shops and office space. Where Roppongi Hills boasts the Grand Hyatt, Midtown has the five-star Ritz Carlton, while in answer to the Mori Art Museum, Midtown has the Suntory Museum of Art's fine collection of traditional Japanese art as well as the 21_21 Design Sight gallery and workshop, a collaboration between architect Tadao Ando and fashion designer Issey Miyake that showcases modern Japanese design.

In fact, a large part of Roppongi's 21st-century renaissance has been artistic. In the same year that Tokyo Midtown was opened, so too came the National Art Center, a cavernous facility designed by Metabolist Movement founder Kisho Kurokawa. Soon after that came the now-annual art extravaganza, Roppongi Art Night, an evening in March during which most of the area's art venues open through the night and art events take place indoors and outdoors across Roppongi.

Roppongi's more traditional nighttime functions are still very much in force, too. Roppongi Hills and Tokyo Midtown both added to the area's culinary credentials, each with a range of chic restaurants and bars, but out in the streets Roppongi also teems with restaurants offering everything from fine traditional Japanese cuisine in places like the three-star Michelin restaurant Ryugin to international flavors, cocktail bars, brew pubs and simple *izakaya*. The raucous side of Roppongi has not waned much either. Partying through the night in well-known venues like Gas Panic, Muse and New Lex Tokyo, among many other clubs, is still high on the agenda of many visitors, and, if anything, stories of drink spiking and credit card scams in some of Roppongi's more insalubrious nightclubs and bars has just added to the area's seamy side in recent years.

RIGHT A café inside Tokyo Midtown.
BELOW The Roppongi Crossing. Before the area was transformed by Roppongi Hills and Tokyo Midtown, this was considered Roppongi's center point and the place to meet friends before heading off into Roppongi's then mostly raucous clubs and bars.

TOKYO TOWER

If towers had feelings, you could hardly blame Tokyo Tower for forlornly looking northeast across the city toward Tokyo Skytree and wondering if its time was up. Before the construction of the 634-meter Skytree, which commenced in the summer of 2008 and finished four years later, the 333-meter Tokyo Tower was not just the tallest structure in Japan but was also one of Tokyo's star tourist attractions, for local tourists at least.

When Tokyo Tower was built in 1958 at a then cost of 3 billion yen to function as a broadcasting tower, it instantly became the standout symbol of Tokyo, its now iconic Eiffel Tower-inspired lattice frame, painted white and international orange (in the case of Tokyo Tower a color often mistaken for red), dominating Tokyo's skyline. Its observation decks, a main observatory at 150 meters and a special observatory at 223.5 meters, gave visitors then unparalleled 360-degree panoramic views of Tokyo, reaching as far as snow-capped Mount Fuji on a clear day.

Looking downward, Tokyo Tower also gave Tokyoites a new perspective on one of the city's most venerable temples, neighboring Zojo-ji. Only the main gateway today hints at its past glory, but

LEFT Tokyo Tower, the original landmark of post-war Japan. **RIGHT** There are many bigger and bolder structures in Tokyo today, but Tokyo Tower still remains an iconic sight.

RIGHT The main hall at Zojo-ji Temple. Like almost all of Zojo-ji's structures, the hall is a modern rebuild. The only structure remaining from the temple's Edo days is the imposing Sangedatsu-mon Gate. Literally meaning the gate (*mon*) for getting delivered (*gedatsu*) from three (*san*) earthly states of man (those being greed, anger and stupidity), the vermilion lacquered 21-meter-high, 28.7-meter-wide gate was built in 1622 during the reign of the second Edo shogun, Tokugawa Hidetada.

in the Edo era, when Zojo-ji served as a family temple of the ruling Tokugawas, some 3,000 priests and novices would have called the then 85,000-square meter complex and its 48 subtemples and 150 or so seminaries home. Much like how Zojo-ji Temple once reflected the Tokugawa's power, several hundred years on, and less than 15 years after much of Tokyo lay in the rubble of World War II, Tokyo Tower was a potent symbol of the city's (and Japan's) rebirth.

Some things change, but not all. The attractions at its base—a waxwork museum and aquarium—are not the most contemporary or alluring by current Tokyo standards. And the bent tip the tower received during the prolonged shaking that hit Tokyo during the Great East Japan Earthquake of March 2011 has admittedly damaged its form a little. Nevertheless, when you see Tokyo Tower now, whether looking up from its base through the lattice framework or seeing it illuminated at night rising tall above the urban sprawl that surrounds it, it is still a striking structure. Thinking about it, Tokyo Skytree may have the better views and the most visitors, and some would say it is architecturally more impressive, too, but Tokyo Tower really should have no reason to feel melancholy.

DAIKANYAMA, EBISU, MEGURO AND SHINAGAWA

If you had to pick a single word to describe much of southern Tokyo, "wealthy" would be high on many Tokyoites' lists, and perhaps nowhere is more representative of that than Daikanyama. With a prime yet quiet, sometimes described as "village-like", location about 1.5 kilometers south of Shibuya, for many Daikanyama is the most chic, sophisticated face of modern Tokyo, a high-end residential area dotted with embassies, trendy boutiques, expensive cosmopolitan restaurants and mellow cafés, not to mention the Fumihiko Maki-designed Hillside Terrace, which with its combination of art spaces, fashionable stores and continental restaurants and cafés has become a defining Daikanyama address.

RIGHT The Daikanyama area is defined by quiet shaded streets, small boutiques and fashionable cafés and bistros.

Move to the nearby Ebisu, Nakameguro and Meguro neighborhoods and the rents do not get any less outrageous. Just south of Daikanyama, Nakameguro is more about hip fashions, bars and bohemian hangouts, a place where "used" is "retro" and costs more than new. East, in Ebisu, the streets have a more familiar Tokyo look and feel to them, except for the standout Yebisu Garden Place complex. With the 39-floor Yebisu Tower at its center, this smart urban redevelopment includes not just the Tokyo headquarters of Sapporo Beer, the company behind it, but also a Westin Hotel, photography museum, shopping arcade, stylish restaurants and boutiques, Yebisu Beer museum, beer hall and other attractions.

A station south from Ebisu, Meguro continues in a similar vein, although with more varied sites of note in the mix. As well as a cluster of historically relevant temples,

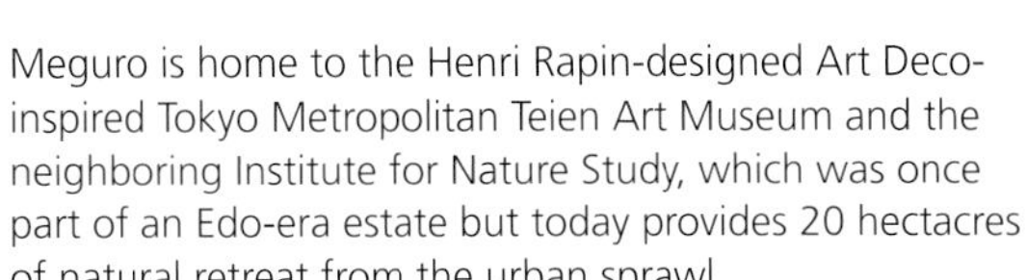

Meguro is home to the Henri Rapin-designed Art Deco-inspired Tokyo Metropolitan Teien Art Museum and the neighboring Institute for Nature Study, which was once part of an Edo-era estate but today provides 20 hectacres of natural retreat from the urban sprawl.

Further eastward comes Shinagawa, which to most Tokyoites has come to mean office blocks, hotels and hub station, crucially with a *shinkansen* stop. Historically, however, Shinagawa is far more interesting. The area was once home to the Takanawa-mon, the main gateway to old Edo and a checkpoint on the Tokaido highway that ran to Kyoto. It is also home to the still intact Sengaku-ji Temple, which came to prominence almost a hundred years after being built in 1612 because of its role in the tale of the 47 Ronin.

The popular tale of samurai loyalty and vengeance, which has found its way into *bunraku* and *kabuki* plays and to the silver screen, tells the story of a group of samurai left leaderless, thereby becoming *ronin*, masterless samurai, when their master Lord Asano is forced to commit ritual suicide after being tricked into drawing his sword on a court official, the villain of the tale, called Lord Kira. After two years of laying low and planning their revenge, the 47 *ronin* returned to kill Lord Kira, then took his severed head and placed it on their master's grave at Sengaku-ji before turning themselves into the authorities. After the 47 were ordered to commit ritual suicide, they were buried in Sengaku-ji alongside their avenged master.

OPPOSITE ABOVE In spring, the 800 or so cherry blossom trees lining the Meguro River burst into pink. At night, with lanterns illuminating the riverside and numerous food and drink vendors set up, the river is among Tokyo's most attractive *hanami* (cherry blossom viewing) spots.

TOP RIGHT The Yebisu Garden Place complex in Ebisu.
ABOVE A Daikanyama café.
BELOW It is not just Shinagawa that still has connections to its past. The Kyu Asakura House in Daikanyama is an Important Cultural Property built in 1919 for politician Torajiro Asakura.

ODAIBA

The man-made island of Odaiba has become the most action-packed, family-friendly destination in Tokyo in recent years, home to attractions that range from hot spring baths to amusement parks and slick museums to mega malls. Yet, it was not all that long ago that Odaiba was just another unspectacular chunk of land reclaimed from Tokyo Bay.

The island started life as part of a series of Edo-era canon batteries built to defend Tokyo against US naval threats in the 1850s, but then lay largely ignored (used for industrial purposes only) until the late 1980s when the Tokyo Metropolitan Government decided to transform it into a futuristic commercial and residential district. With the kind of indiscriminate spending that characterized Japan's bubble economy, by the mid-1990s in excess of one trillion yen had been thrown into Odaiba's redevelopment, most notably on the construction of the Rainbow Bridge and Yurikamome transit system, which now connect Odaiba to central Tokyo.

Despite the bubble economy having burst in rather spectacular fashion in late 1991 and early 1992, asset prices tumbling and signaling the start of what has been dubbed Japan's "lost decade", in the mid- and late 1990s things began to take off in Odaiba. Tokyo Big Sight, the city's leading convention center and one of its most distinctive pieces of architecture thanks to the four inverted pyramids that serve as its support pillars, was opened in 1996, and followed a year later by the equally striking Kenzo Tange-designed offices of Fuji TV.

The developments came thick and fast after that: an artificial beach (albeit one you would probably need a shot for, if you swam off it), a replica of the Statue of Liberty, mall after mall, a giant Ferris wheel, cutting-

FAR LEFT Rainbow Bridge and Odaiba's version of the Statue of Liberty. Although the replica of the statue looks huge in this image, it is only one-tenth the size of the US original.
BELOW The Tokyo Big Sight convention and exhibition center.

edge amusement centers and amusement parks, the brilliant Museum of Emerging Science & Innovation, an Edo-themed hot spring resort and, more recently, a small Legoland, Madame Tussauds and an 18-meter-high statue of a robot from the Gundam *manga/ anime* series.

As for what comes next for Odaiba, that will be of Olympic proportions. Tokyo Big Sight will host the wrestling, taekwondo and fencing events at the Tokyo 2020 Olympic Games, while kayaking, mountain biking and rowing events will also be held on Odaiba, with many other events nearby in the other parts of the bay area. Odaiba will have an Olympic legacy to add to its Edo roots.

TOP The offices of Fuji TV framed by the Aomi-Daiba Crosswalk (pedestrian bridge).
LEFT The Gundam statue in front of the Diver City Tokyo mall.

ABOVE One of many shopping malls on Odaiba, the Venus Fort mall is designed along Renaissance Italy themes and, for reasons unknown, features a sky-like ceiling that moves and changes color during the day.

WESTERN TOKYO

Nakanosakaue
Nakanosakau
Oedo Line
Higashi-shinjuku
Seibu-Shinjuku
KABUKI-CHO
Kawadacho
Ichigaya-yanagicho
Yochomachi
Ichigaya-yakuojimachi
Ichigaya-kagacho
Ome-kaido
Nishi-shinjuku
Golden Gai
Meiji-dori
Sumiyoshicho
Ichigaya-nakanocho
Gyoen-dori
Ichigaya-daimachi
Tomihisacho
Ichigay honmura
Tocho-dori
Kita-dori
Togo Seiji Art Museum
Shinjuku-nishiguchi
Shinjuku
Akebonobashi
EAST SHINJUKU
Yasukuni-dori
Shinjuku Line
Nishi-shinjuku-gochome
Tochomae
Chuo-dori
Shinjuku-sanchome
SHINJUKU STATION
Information Bureau of Tokyo
Funamachi
Sakamachi
Juniso-dori
Gijido-dori
Higashi-dori
Shinjuku Skyscraper District
Aizumicho
Arakicho
Shinjuku Historical Museum
Honshiocho
SHINJUKU CHUO PARK
Koen-dori
Tokyo Metropolitan Gov't Bldg
Tokyo Toy Museum
Shobo Museum
San'eicho
Shinjuku-dori
Shinjuku-gyoenmae
Honan-dori
Minami-dori
Koshu-Kaido
Yotsuya-sanchome
Marunouchi Line
Naitomachi
Samoncho
Yamate-dori
Bunka Gakuen Costume Museum
SHINJUKU GYOEN GARDEN
Yotsuya
Japanese Style Court
English Style Court
Daikyocho
Sugacho
Yoyogi
Minami-shinjuku
Noguchi Hideyo Memorial Hall
Tokyo Opera City
HONMACHI
European Style Court
Shinanomachi
Art Gallery
Hatsudai
Minami-Motomachi
Japanese Sword Museum
Sendagaya
Shinanomachi
MINAMIMOTOMACHI PARK
Shuto E'way No.4 Shinjuku Line
Kokuritsu-kyogijo
Tokyo Metropolitan Gymnasium
Sangubashi
Kitasando
Prince Chichibu Memorial Sports Museum
Seitoku Memorial Picture Gallery
AKASAKA DETACHED PAL
MEIJI INNER GARDEN
HATSUDAI
Keio Line
Kasumigaokamachi
MOTO-AKASAKA
Odakyu Line
MEIJI PARK
THE MEIJI OUTER GARDEN
Oedo Line
AKASAKA DETACHED PALACE GA
Meiji Shrine
Yoyogi-kamizonocho
IRIS GARDEN
Otorii
Aoyama-itchome
NISHIHARA
Galen-nishi-dori
Ginkgo Avenue (Icho Namiki)
Chichibunomiya Rugby Stadium
Hanzomon & Ginza Line
Moto-yoyogicho
Harajuku
Takesita-dori
Yoyogi Park
Ota Museum of Ukiyo-e Prints
Ura-Harajuku (Cat Street)
Watari-Um Museum
Gaiemmae
Yoyogi-uehara
Yoyogi-hachiman
Forever 21
H&M
Meiji-jingumae
La Foret
Kita-Aoyama
Yoyogi-koen
Zara
HARAJUKU CROSSING
Omotesando
NOGI PARK
Harajuku
Levi's
Omotesando Hills
UEHARA
YOYOGI NATIONAL GYMNASIUM
Dior
Aoyama
Aoyama-dori
21_21 De Sight Mu
Omotesando-dori
Nogizaka
TOMIGAYA
Burberry
Paul Stuart
Louis Vuitton
Armani
AOYAMA CEMETERY
Suntory Museum of Art
Inokashira-dori
Koen-dori
Meiji-dori
Gucci
OMOTESANDO CROSSING
Galen-nishi-dori
Galen-higashi-dori
Museum of Modern Japan Literature
Kamiyamacho
Tobacco and Salt Museum
Tepco Electric Energy Museum
Tessenkai Noh Theater
Prada
National Art Center
AOYAMA PARK
ROPPO CROSS
KOMABA PARK
Former Marquis Maeda's House
Toguri Museum of Art
Organ-zaka
Marui
Parco
MIYASHITA PARK
Nezu Museum
Okamoto Taro Memorial Museum
Japan Folk Crafts Museum
SHOTO
The Museum
Bunkamura-dori
Seibu
Shibuya
Kotto-dori
Mori Art Museum
ROPPONGI HILL
109
Hachiko Statue
Shibuya Hikarie
Komaba-todaimae
Shoto Art Museum
Sakae-dori
DOGENZAKA
SHIBUYA STATION
Roppongi-dori
N
KOMABANO PARK
KOMABA
Maruyamacho
Tokyu Plaza
Meiji-dori
Shinsencho
Shinsen
Inokashira Line
Shibuya Ward Museum
MOTO-AZABU
DAIZAWA
500 m
1000 feet
scale 1 : 25 000
Tokyu Den'entoshi Line
Sakuragaoka-cho
Nanpeidaicho
Miki Takeo Memorial Museum
Yamatane Museum of Art
OHASHI
Uguisudanicho
HIRO-O

TOKYO'S WESTERN DISTRICTS

Western Tokyo, or rather the western part of Tokyo's 23 central wards, does not fit easily under a single definition. While Tokyo's east side is uniformly more traditional, or at least has not strayed very far from its working-class roots, the west is more eclectic. Omotesando, the chic boulevard that leads toward the tranquility and calm of Meiji Jingu Shrine, is all about high-end fashion and modern architecture, while neighboring Harajuku and nearby Shibuya both exude a youthful exuberance that is at its most stylish in the back streets of Ura-Harajuku and most colorful and vibrant in the teen boutiques along Harajuku's cramped Takeshita-dori and in Shibuya's 109 building. Shinjuku is different again, comprising a patchwork of contrasts, from the high-rise business district on its west side to the red lights of the Kabuki-cho area on its east.

OMOTESANDO AND HARAJUKU

Walking along Omotesando-dori is like taking in a slide show of Europe's most prestigious fashion houses. Armani, Burberry, Dior, Gucci, Louis Vuitton, Paul Stuart and Prada all have sleekly designed stores on the zelkova-lined boulevard, as do other high-end brands of that type. Yet, a hundred years ago, when Omotesando-dori first began to take shape, it was intended for a more solemn purpose, functioning as the approach to Meiji Jingu Shrine (page 88), which was built in the Taisho era (1912–26) to enshrine the souls of the then recently deceased Emperor Meiji and Empress Shoken.

Given his Western-influenced efforts at breaking free from Edo-era isolation and at modernizing Japan, one cannot help but think the Emperor Meiji might enjoy the modern architecture that now helps define Omotesando-dori. It was, after all, during his time on the Chrysanthemum Throne in the latter half of the 1800s and early 1900s that the first European-style buildings began to appear in central Tokyo.

Fast forward to recent times and buildings like Tod's, a slim L-shaped structure encased in an enclosure of sharply angled concrete elements and polygonal glass plates that was designed by 2013 Pritzker Prize winner Toyo Ito, have made Omotesando-dori one of Tokyo's most architecturally striking streets. And now dominating the street more than any other structure, since it was completed in 2006, is the Tadao Ando-designed Omotesando Hills, which at 250 meters long stretches along almost a quarter of Omotesando-dori's entire length.

The internationally acclaimed Ando, known for his stark use of concrete, wood and natural lighting and an ability to blend his designs into their surrounding environments, most notably

LEFT The Tadao Ando-designed Omotesando Hills mall redefined Omotesando-dori when it opened in 2006.

OPPOSITE LEFT The Toyo Ito-designed Tod's building is one of Omotesando's architectural standouts. **OPPOSITE RIGHT** Omotesando Hills runs almost 250 meters along Omotesando-dori. Although a modern architectural tour de force, Tadao Ando also incorporated some history into the structure, retaining part of the 1920s-built apartments that made way for Hills.

LEFT The Tokyo Metro exits on to the zelkova-lined Omotesando-dori at Omotesando Station. RIGHT Harajuku Crossing reflecting in the kaleidoscope of mirrors that surround the entrance to the Tokyu Plaza Omotesando Harajuku building, or Omohara for short.

ABOVE A couple of cosplayers stand by the ticket gates to Harajuku Station. Akihabara is the center of all things *otaku* (geeky) and *anime*- or *manga*-related in Japan, but the Harajuku area is also a popular hangout for cosplayers and anyone else into dressing up.
ABOVE RIGHT Harajuku Station on the JR Yamanote Line.
RIGHT Harajuku is known as much for its stylish youthful fashions as it is for its quirky styles.

gave Hills a six-level atrium that reaches three stories above ground and three below, with a spiraling ramp connecting the different levels. But if you look at the building's southeast end, you will also notice a nod from Ando to Omotesando's past in the form of a section of an old tenement building incorporated into the design, part of the charming but run down 1920s-built Dojunkai Apartments that were torn down, to substantial public outcry, to make way for Omotesando Hills.

Away from the main stretch of Omotesando-dori, a web of side streets brings a distinct change of atmosphere. Gone are the luxury brands, replaced by a youthful and more vibrant kind of style. Walk along Ura-Harajuku (aka Cat Street), which cuts across Omotesando-dori, and the boutiques of young local designers rub shoulders with small cafés and the occasional used clothing store. That serves as a taste of what is to come further up Omotesando-dori when the road reaches the Harajuku Crossing. With a young, trend-following kind of shopper in mind, overseas brands like Zara, Levi's, Forever 21 and H&M compete here with oddly named local boutiques (the "Jane Marple" store sadly does not specialize in tweed jackets for septuagenarian sleuths), a hundred or so housed in the La Foret Harajuku department store alone and even more lining Harajuku's most recognizable street, Takeshita-dori, where Harajuku's trendier street fashions make way for cosplay stores, places selling teen idol merchandise and Tokyo's most playful teen fashions.

ABOVE Style in Harajuku cuts across a broad range of subcultures, from punks to cosplayers to goths and many other points in between.
LEFT The seemingly always crowded Takeshita-dori in Harajuku. Home to numerous fashion and accessory stores aimed predominantly at teens, there are few places better to check out the more colorful and radical youth trends of the day.

MEIJI SHRINE AND YOYOGI PARK

Passing under Meiji Jingu Shrine's three grand torii gateways, walking along gravel pathways shaded by towering forest, it can be hard to believe you are just a few minutes' walk from Harajuku and the teen crowds of Takeshita-dori. Built in the 1910s to enshrine the souls of the Emperor Meiji, under whose reign (1868–1912) Japan transitioned from feudal state to modern world power, and his consort Empress Shoken, the shrine and its 28-hectare forest is a sea of calm and tradition set aside an otherwise pulsating expression of relentlessly modern Japan.

While on weekends Harajuku's station front area might be overrun by teens in blood-splattered gothic outfits, Meiji Jingu might see a Shinto wedding procession gracefully moving through the grounds, briefly capturing the interest of visitors writing wishes on votive plaques they then hang on racks in front of the main shrine.

Adjoining Meiji Shrine is Yoyogi Park, once the location of US military barracks known as Washington Heights during the occupation of Japan and later, in 1964, the site of the main athletes village during the Tokyo Olympics. The remnants of the Olympics, or the "legacy" to use recent Olympic parlance, are still in use in the park. The 48,000-seat National Stadium, the main venue for the 1964 Olympics, today hosts J-League soccer matches, while the 25,000-seat Chichibunomiya Rugby Stadium and the Tokyo Metropolitan Gymnasium are also major sporting facilities.

More importantly, since Yoyogi took its current shape as a public park in 1967, it has become one of the most vibrant public spaces in Tokyo. Visit on a weekend and you could well find yourself in the middle of a festival. Events like the annual Thai Festival, One Love Jamaica and Earth Day celebrations are held here, while music events frequently take place on the open-air stage in the park's southern end.

If there is nothing major going on, then you could stop to watch the buskers and rockabilly dancers that descend on the park on weekends, or head to the northern side of the park to picnic with Tokyoites in search of a rare moment of green-tinted peace and quiet among the park's expanse of lawns and trees. What will become of the park now that Tokyo has been awarded the 2020 Games? Will, as some Tokyoites fear, Yoyogi's green spaces be sacrificed to expand or replace the current sporting facilities? It is anybody's guess, but for the time being Yoyogi Park combines with Meiji Shrine to give Tokyo a very welcome urban oasis.

LEFT Before entering the grounds of a shrine, it is tradition to purify oneself by rinsing one's hands and mouth at the shrine's purification fountain.

BELOW A Shinto wedding procession makes its way through the inner shrine area, with the bride and groom together under the red umbrella.

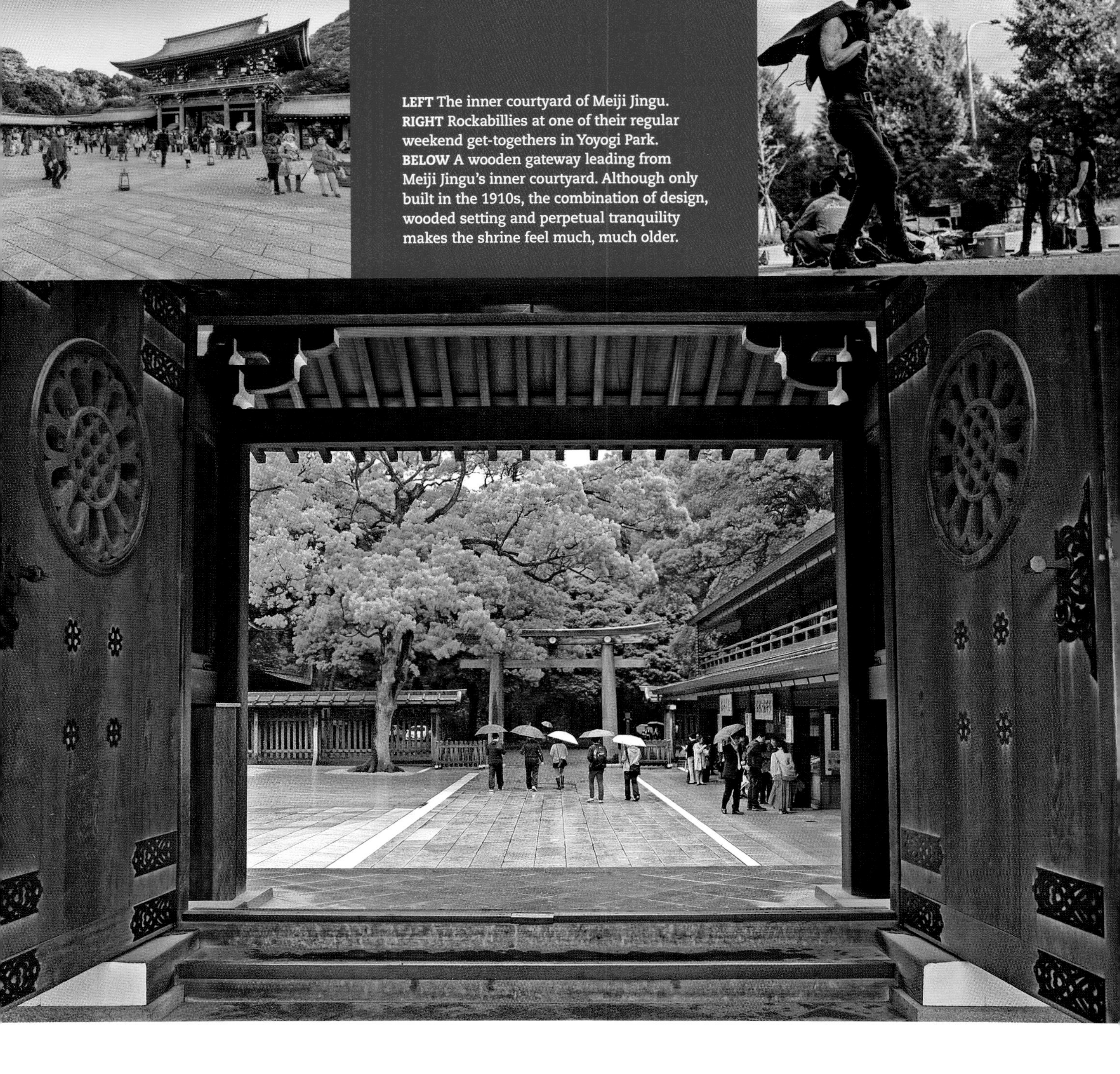

LEFT The inner courtyard of Meiji Jingu.
RIGHT Rockabillies at one of their regular weekend get-togethers in Yoyogi Park.
BELOW A wooden gateway leading from Meiji Jingu's inner courtyard. Although only built in the 1910s, the combination of design, wooded setting and perpetual tranquility makes the shrine feel much, much older.

LEFT There is a very good chance of seeing colorful costumes and quirky fashions on any trip to Shibuya, including during Halloween.
RIGHT Shibuya's youthfulness and the political engagement of Tokyo's youth is reflected in the area's graffiti. After the earthquake, tsunami and nuclear accident of March 2011, stickers of the "I hate rain" girl pictured here in the raincoat began popping up on Shibuya's walls as part of anti-nuke protests.

SHIBUYA

Shibuya is many things: a center of nightlife and fashion, home to the most iconic and busiest street crossing in the country, and the setting for Japan's most endearing tale of loyalty. The latter is a good place to start because the canine protagonist sits just outside Shibuya Station.

The dog in question, an Akita inu called Hachiko, waits by the station exit now named after him, cast in bronze, left ear bent over, right ear pricked up, in the place he used to wait each day almost 90 years ago for his master, a professor at the University of Tokyo, to return from work. What makes this particular dog so famous is, that after his master did not come home one day in May 1925 (he had suffered a cerebral hemorrhage at work and died), Hachiko nevertheless kept coming back to the station at the same time every day to greet his master off the train. After seven years of repeating this routine, his story eventually found its way into the *Asahi Shinbum* newspaper, thus assuring his fame.

The story of Hachiko, known as *chuuken Hachiko* or "faithful dog Hachiko", resonates so strongly with the Japanese that not only was the dog honored by the statue in 1934 (and he was present for the unveiling!), but after his death a year later his body was stuffed and put on exhibition at the National Museum of Nature and Science in Ueno, where it still resides. He has even had his story made into

OPPOSITE It gets called a few things: the Shibuya Crossing, the Shibuya Scramble, mayhem. Either way, the crossing at the heart of Shibuya has become one of Tokyo's most photographed spots as people descend upon it from all sides.

RIGHT The now iconic statue of Hachiko the dog by Shibuya Station. The statue is a popular meeting point, but on a weekday night or weekend finding a friend in the crowds around it can be like finding the proverbial needle in a haystack.

FAR RIGHT Another well-known meeting point in Shibuya is this old rail carriage just across from Hachiko. Like Hachiko, hanging out here for a while provides the perfect vantage point for absorbing Shibuya's fashions, styles and vibe.

ABOVE The Shibuya Crossing of an evening. **BELOW** Shibuya's Center-Gai area.

movies, including an eminently miss-able Westernized version starring Richard Gere.

The crowds that flow past Hachiko today, on their way toward the Shibuya Crossing from where they break like a wave over Shibuya's main shopping areas, are generally a young bunch, certainly much younger than the crowds of Ginza. Over the last couple of decades, the Shibuya area has become, along with neighboring Harajuku, Tokyo's most vibrant youth center, where Tokyoites in their teens and early twenties come to party, shop and soak up the latest trends and fashions. With the focus varying from techno and house to K-pop, Shibuya is home to many of Tokyo's best clubs, while buildings like 109 (pronounced *ichi maru kyu*), an eight-floor collection of more than 100 small fashion boutiques, and the nearby Center-Gai shopping precinct are a barometer for gauging the latest fashion trends.

That is not to say that Shibuya does not also reach out to a broader selection of consumers. It does, with major department stores like Marui, Tokyu, Seibu and Parco, and one of Tokyo's latest major urban redevelopments, the 34-story Shibuya Hikarie, which has loomed large over the east side of Shibuya Station since 2012, enticing a more mature and more affluent shopper than Center-Gai and 109, with a combination of slickly designed retail spaces, cafés, restaurants, art and cultural venues, and more.

ABOVE The Shibuya Crossing.
BELOW Fashions come and go with a ferocious regularity in Shibuya. How many people will actually remember when oddly matched tights were "in"?

ABOVE The Shibuya 109 building. Like Takeshita-dori and the La Foret building in Harajuku, a walk around 109 provides an insight into the very latest youth fashions and trends in Tokyo. Geared to young women, 109's eight floors house a hundred or so small boutiques that together cover a variety of youthful styles and numerous local and international brands.

SHINJUKU

Where to begin with Shinjuku? Maybe we could start by talking about its station, which, with more than 3.5 million people passing through its 36 platforms daily is one of the busiest in the world. Or maybe we should begin with the high-rise business district on the station's west side, where the 45-story twin towers of the Kenzo Tange-designed Tokyo Metropolitan Government Building dominate the skyline and on clear days provide breath-taking views of Mount Fuji from its observation decks. We could even begin somewhere that belies Shinjuku's neon-lit, crowded and unflinchingly energetic reputation—Shinjuku Gyoen.

Although only a 10-minute walk from Shinjuku Station, Shinjuku Gyoen feels entirely removed from the city. Part of that is down to the peace and quiet that enshrouds the park's 56-hectare grounds, but mostly the sense of seclusion comes from the rich natural surrounds, which have been manipulated since the Edo era (when for a while the park was part of a *daimyo*'s residence) with a combination of traditional Japanese garden design, English landscaping and formal French styles.

In spring, in particular, when the fleeting front of cherry blossoms that sweeps northwest across Japan briefly paints Shinjuku Gyoen a palette of delicate pinks, there is nowhere better in Tokyo for *hanami* (cherry blossom viewing). In summer, the grounds are then transformed by lush green foliage punctuated by varicolored rose beds, before autumn brings rich, earthy tones and fallen leaves carpet the sprawling lawns.

As calming as Shinjuku Gyoen is, more representative of Shinjuku, which for many is the epitome of modern, brash Tokyo, are

OPPOSITE ABOVE The JR Chuo/Sobu Line is one of many that serve Shinjuku Station, helping make it one of the busiest stations in the world.
OPPOSITE BELOW The small, rough and ready *izakaya* and restaurants in Omoide Yokocho (lit. Memory Lane) near Shinjuku Station's West Exit capture the old Tokyo vibe like nowhere else.

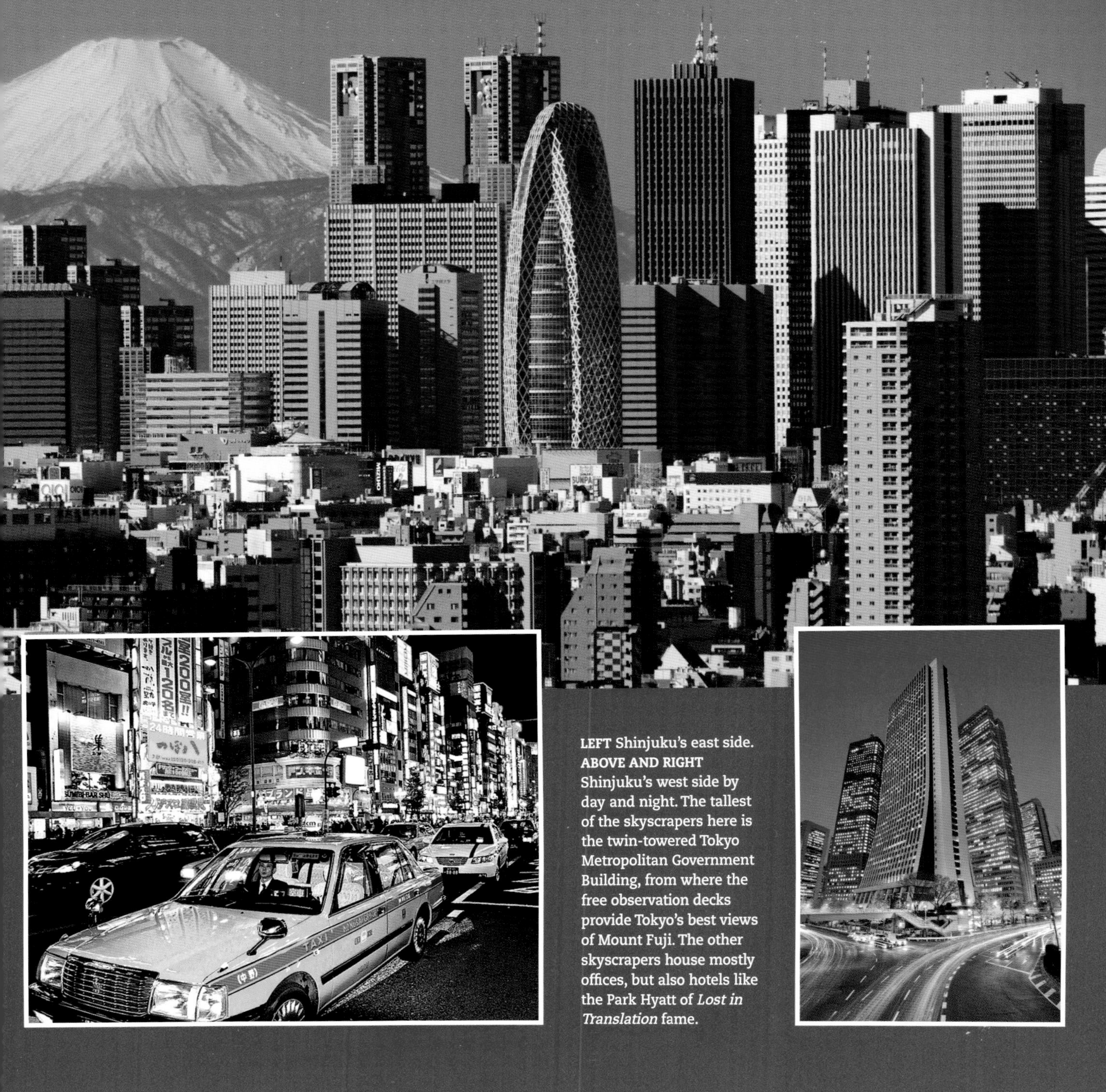

LEFT Shinjuku's east side. **ABOVE AND RIGHT** Shinjuku's west side by day and night. The tallest of the skyscrapers here is the twin-towered Tokyo Metropolitan Government Building, from where the free observation decks provide Tokyo's best views of Mount Fuji. The other skyscrapers house mostly offices, but also hotels like the Park Hyatt of *Lost in Translation* fame.

RIGHT Shinjuku Gyoen accented by cherry blossoms in spring. The garden is one of Tokyo's best and especially so in the *hanami* (cherry blossom viewing) season.

BELOW From tiny back-street eateries to bohemian bars, come nightfall Shinjuku has some of the best places in Tokyo for after work dinner and drinks.

OPPOSITE ABOVE The entrance to the Kabuki-cho area. As the name suggests, the initial plan was for Kabuki-cho to be a theater district, but instead it ended up becoming Tokyo's most notorious red-light district.

the bustling shopping areas on the south and east sides of the station, home to a mix of department stores, high-end boutiques, budget fashion chains, sporting goods stores and home electronics stores. But even more than that, it is what happens to Shinjuku after dark that best defines the area.

Kabuki-cho, Tokyo's most notorious red-light district, is just a five-minute walk from Shinjuku Station's east exit, and although its reputation was built on sex clubs and *yakuza*-owned establishments, Kabuki-cho is also home to many above-board bars, *izakaya* and restaurants. Next door to that things get even more interesting in the Golden-Gai area, a collection of narrow lanes filled with tiny, often quirky bars (think baroque interiors, hospital themes and owners obsessed with 1960s rock and soul) that over the years have built a reputation for being the watering holes of Tokyo's literati and other creative types. Then there is the nearby "Little Asia" area, around Okubu and Shin-Okubu stations, a focal point for Tokyo's Korean community and the best place to try not just Korean food but also Southeast Asian. When put together, the result is Japan's most varied and colorful district—a captivating melting pot.

ABOVE The range of eating and drinking options in Shinjuku is fantastic. Casual Japanese counter-style joints like this one abound, as do larger *izakaya*, Korean restaurants, Chinese restaurants, Southeast Asian flavors and numerous pubs and bars.

AROUND
TOKYO

to Fukushima
to Iwaki
Nikko Nat. Park
Tosho-gu-Shrine
Nikko
Shioya
Yaita
Yamatsuri
Kitaiba
Minakami Hot Spring
Katashina
Yudanaka Hot Spring
Joshinetsu-kogen Nat. Park
Hoppo Hot Spring
Kidoike Hot Spring
Minakami
Kawaba
JR Joetsu Line
Joetsu Shinkansen
JR Nikko Line
Tohoku Shinkansen
JR Tohoku Line
Sakura
Daigo
Nakagawa
Takahagi
JR Suigun Line
Nasukarasuyama
Kumanoya Hot Spring
Yunotaira Hot Spring
Nakanojo
Numata
Ashio Mountains
Okamoto
Ichikai
Gozen'yama
Hitachi
Tsumagoi
Agatsuma Line
Higashiagatsuma
Komochi
Akagi
Azuma
Akagi-Shrine
Kurohone
Awano
Kanuma
Utsunomiya
Haga
Hitachi-Ota
Naganohara
Kawarayu Hot Spring
Ikaho
Hanawa
Nishikata
Tatara
Motegi
Hitachi Omiya
Omika
Shinkazawa Hot Spring
Shibukawa
Kitatachibana
Fujimi
Suzumenomiya
Nanakai
Urizura
Hara Museum of Contemporary Art
Yoshioka
Tsuga
Mashiko
Saimyo-ji
Johoku
Naka
JR Joban Line
Takamine Hot Spring
Nagano Shinkansen
Shinto
Maebashi
Ogo
Gumma
Kasukawa
Kasakane
Kiryu
Ishibashi
Moka
Ishizukayakushi-ji
Shinmaebashi
Akabori
Yabuzukahonmachi
Kuzu
Tochigi
Kokubunji
Ninomiya
Iwase
Kasama
Hitachinaka
Ajigaura
Isozaki-misaki
Mito
Karuizawa
Takasaki
Matsuida
Annaka
Isesaki
Azuma
Orihime-Shrine
Ashikaga
Ohira
Minamikawachi
Kasama-inari
Nakaminato
Oarai
to Nagano
Awano
Mito Line
Amabiki-kannon
Shinmachi
Oyama
Ota
L. Hinuma
Oarai Coast
Saku
Myogi
Tomioka
Kanra
Yoshi
Honjo
Ojima
Oizumi
Fujioka
Makabe
Iwama
Ibaraki
Fujioka
Tansho
Okabe
Menuma
Itakura
Nogi
Sanwa
Tsukubasan-shrine
Suigo-Tsukuba Q.N.P.
Omitama
Shimonita
Fukaya
Morin-ji
Kodama
Chiyoda
Meiwa
Koga
Asahi
PACIFIC OCEAN
Kamiizumi
Minamikawara
Hanyu
Kitakawabe
Yachiyo
Ishioka
Onishi
Kurihashi
Chiyoda
Sakuho
Nagatoro
Kawamoto
Sashima
Niihari
Tamari
Nakasato
Koumi
Nagatoro Valley
Washimiya
Ishige
Tsukuba
Dejima
Taiyo
JR Koumi Line
Minano
Ueno
Ogawa
Kuki
Bando
Tsuchiura
Hozaki-Kanno
Royal Ocean
Higashichichibu
Ranzan
Satte
Kitaura
L. Kasumigaura
L. Kitaura
Ogano
Mitsukaido
Aso
Minamiaiki
Higashima-tsuyama
Suigo-Tsukuba Q.N.P.
Chichibu
Sekiyado
Joban Line
Nammoku
Yokoze
Sakado
L. Ushikunuma
Ushibori
Kashima
Kawakami
Mitsumineguchi
Iwatsuki
Moriya
Inashiki
Chichibutama N.P.
Tsurugashima
Ushiku
Mitsuminesancho
Omiya
Kawagoe
Saitama
Yoshikawa
Ryugasaki
Abiko
Kamisu
Fujimi
Urawa
Nagareyama
Ikasu-Shrine
Narita Line
Sawara
Wild Duck
Tabayama
Sayama
Misato
Kashiwa
Iruma
Okutamako
Hanno
Asaka
Kawaguchi
Soka
Kioroshi
Inzai
Shinsho-ji
Kurimoto
Sasagawa
to Nagano
Tokorozawa
Yasio
L. Imba-numa
Kitatsuru
Niiza
Matsudo
Narita
Yamada
Hazaki
Yokota Air Base
Wako
Kosuge
Ichikawa
L. Imba-numa
Imba
Tako
Higata
Yamanashi
Nakano
Yachiyo
Narita International Airport
Enzan
Akishima
Kichijoji
Sosa
Kai
Kofu
Hajima
Yachiyodai
Katsunuma
Koganei
TOKYO
Funabashi
Yokaichiba
Hachioji
Sobu Line
Fuchu
Narashino
Sagamiko
Tokyo Disney Sea
Yasashigaura
Sasago
Uenohara
Tokyo Disney Land
Chiba
Sanmu
Chuo
JR Chuo Line
Otsuki
Sagamihara
Kujukurihama
Togane
Tsuru
Doshi
Machida
Kawasaki
Sotobo Line
Ichikawamisato
Mitsutoge
Ichihara
Honda
Kujukuri
Tokyo International (Haneda) Airport
Minobu
Kawaguchiko
Tanzawa Oyama Q.N.P.
Oami
Fujiyoshida
Fuji Q Highland
Ebina
Yokohama
Goi
Katakai
Yamato
Fuji-Hakone-Izu N.P.
Yamanakako
US Naval Airbase Atsugi
Chinatown
Chiba-kokusai
Shirako
Yamanaka
L. Yamanaka
Atsugi
Kisarazu
Mobara
JR Minobu Line
Sankei Garden
Kazusa-ichinomiya
Hadano
Kimitsu
Kururi Line
Yaga
Yamakita
Isehara
Mt. Fuji 3776m
Oyama
Fujisawa
Yokohama Hakkeijima Sea Paradise
Ichinomiya
PACIFIC OCEAN
Matsuda
Hiratsuka
Daibutsu
Hakone Outdoor Sculpture Museum
Chigasaki
Nambu
Boso Peninsula
Gotenba
Kamakura
Futtsu-koen
Otaki
Oiso Long Beach
Morito
Odawara
Uchibo Line
Kazusa-Nakano
Ohara
Togendai
Yokosuka
Hakone
N
Isumi
Fuji
Susono
Tsukuihama
Miurakaigan
Hamakanaya
Onjuku
Yoshiwara
Katsuura
Miura
Mishima
Sagami Bay
Sotobo Line
Kamogawa
Manazuru Cape
to Nagoya
Hara
Tokaido Shinkansen
Tagonoura
Numazu
Atami
Kyonan
JR Tokaido
Tomiyama
Futomi
20 km
10 mile
Scale 1 : 1,000,000
Ohito
Usami
Maruyama
Wada
Minami Boso Q.N.P.
Sunosaki-Shrine
Shuzenji
Chitose
Ito
Sunosaki Cape
Tateyama
Heda
Shuzenji Hot Spring
Chikura
Suraga Bay
Izu
Kawana
Minami-Chikura
Shirahama
Toi
Fuji-Hakone-Izu N.P.
Kamo

SIDE TRIPS AROUND TOKYO

While most of Tokyo has long since shed the outward expression of its Edo and pre-Edo past, in the outer limits of Greater Tokyo and just beyond lie several fine historic and culturally significant sites, from the temples and shrines of the 13th-century political and spiritual capital Kamakura to the lavish Tosho-gu Shrine complex built in Nikko for the first Edo shogun, Tokugawa Ieyasu. Playing a more recent role in Japan's past is Yokohama, Tokyo's neighbor to the southwest, a fishing village that rapidly blossomed into a thriving international port with the onset of the Meiji era and end of Japan's isolation policy. Not to be forgotten, looking west from Tokyo is Japan's most recognizable natural wonder, Mount Fuji, whose dominating presence has had a profound impact on Japanese culture and spirituality.

YOKOHAMA

You would not guess it looking at Yokohama's swanky waterside development, Minato Mirai 21, and the 70-story Landmark Tower rising from its heart, but 160 years ago there was almost nothing to Yokohama. In 1853, when Commodore Matthew Perry of the US Navy sailed what the Japanese dubbed his "Black Ships" into Tokyo Bay and with it put the wheels in motion toward the signing of a treaty that would end more than 200 years of self-imposed isolation, Yokohama's population was barely in excess of a hundred.

Despite centuries of Edo isolation under the Tokugawa's *sakoku* (lit. chained country) policy, which gradually came into effect during the 1630s and was not completely abolished until the Meiji Restoration of 1868, it did not take long for Yokohama to begin its transformation after the Black Ships first appeared in the bay. Chukagai, Yokohama's Chinatown, was established just a decade after Perry's arrival, and today is one of the city's main draws. The area's 200 or so restaurants, which between them cover almost every variation of Chinese cuisine, and roughly 300 shops that specialize in everything from dumpling steamers to Chinese condiments, combine to pull in some 18 million visitors a year to Chinatown, as well as forming the focal point of a vibrant Chinese community.

ABOVE At 106 meters, the Yokohama Marine Tower has been a bayside landmark since 1961. **RIGHT AND FAR RIGHT** The colorful streets of Yokohama's Chinatown.

LEFT The Yokohama skyline seen from Osanbashi, the main international pier at the Port of Yokohama. The 296-meter Landmark Tower in the Minato Mirai 21 district rises above the historic Akarenga warehouses and Cosmo Clock 21 Ferris wheel, while off to the right is the Yokohama Grand InterContinental Hotel. **RIGHT** Yokohama Bay Bridge. Look closely and you will see the faint silhouette of Mount Fuji in the background.

Pass through Yokohama Station on the *shinkansen* (bullet train) and you would not be able to distinguish the city from central Tokyo. Take time to explore this home to 3.5 million people, however, and you will soon see that Yokohama is proud of its well-preserved past. The waterfront Harbor View Park, where until 1870 British troops had a garrison to protect early foreign settlers and traders, retains several Western-influenced buildings that date to the early Meiji period, while the Gaijin Bochi (Foreigner's Cemetery), a graveyard overlooking the bay that has become a fairly popular site for Japanese tourists, is the resting place for many of the first foreigners to trade with and live in Japan after the arrival of the Black Ships. One of the oldest of the 3,000 graves here is that of Charles Richardson, a British merchant

Yokohama
200 m
500 ft
Scale 1 : 15,000
N
Yokohama Harbor
Sogo
Sogo Museum of Art
Sky Bldg
Minato-Odori
JR Freight Line
YOKOHAMA MINATOMIRAI SPORTS PARK
Keihin Port & Harbor Office
Tsukiji Bridge
Nissan Motor
Fuji Xerox R&D Square
TAKASHIMA CHUO PARK
Ocean Twr
Tide Containing Pond
SEASIDE PARK (RINKO PARK)
Shin-takashima
Gento Yokohama
109 Cinemas
Jonathan's
Blitz
Suzukake-dori
Jackmall East
Foresis L
MM Towers
Pacifico Yokohama Exhibition Hall
INAX Yokohama Showroom
Cosmo World
Media Tower
Jackmall West
Foresis R
Shop Minato Fureai
Super Autobacs
Leaf Minatomirai
Otoya
Keiyu Hospital
PC Depot
Otsuka Kagu
Tsutaya
Minatomirai
National Convention Hall
Anpanman Children's Museum
7Eleven
Minatomirai Center Bldg
Yokohama Minato Mirai Hall
Pier 21
Yokohama Grand InterContinental
den Doso Denki
Home Center Sekichu
Icho-dori
GURAMMORU PARK
Kisoji
Mitsubishi Minatomirai Industrial Museum
Yokohama Museum of Art
Queen's East
Tower C
QUEEN'S SQUARE
Pan Pacific Yokohama Bay
Shinko Futo Kyakusen Terminal
TOYOTA JOY PARK
Minatomirai-Odori
Mitsubishi
Keyaki-dori
Tower B
at! 1st
Tower A
Yokohama Cosmoworld
Yokohama Minatomirai Spa Manyo Club
Japanese Overseas Migration Museum
Sony
Landmark Plaza
Moku-Moku Waku-Waku Yokohama Yo-Yo
Yokohama NS Center Bldg
Uchidacho
Hard Rock
Ferris Wheel/ Yokohama Cosmo World Amusement Park
JICA Yokohama Center
Yokohama Coast Guard Office
Ganki Yokocho
Sirius
Landmark Tower
Dockyard Garden
Kids Carnival Zone
Warner Mycal Cinemas
Japan Coast Guard Museum Yokohama Branch
Bank of Yokohama
Sakura-dori
Royal Park
KFC
McDonalds
Hanasakicho
Viamare
Nippon-Maru
Yokohama World Porters
SHINKO PIER
KAMON-YAMA PARK
Blue Line
Nisseki Yokohama Bldg
Yokohama International Passenger Terminal
Tobe-dori
Noh Theater
Yokohama Port Museum
Navios
Red Brick Park
Kanagawa Pref. Library
Kanagawa Youth Hostel
New Otani Inn
Kitanaka Bridge
Bankokubashi-dori
Shinko
Myogen-ji
Bankoku-bashi Bridge
Daiichi Kowan Government Bldg
Akarenga Soko Shopping Mall
Seishonen Center
Colette Mare
Minato Mirai 21
Silk Exchange
AKA RENGA PARK
Terrace
Ongaku-dori
Kitanakadori
OSANBASHI PIER
Momijigaoka
Hoko-ji
Sakuragicho
Sakuragicho Washington
Yokohama Government Office Building No. 2
Kaigandori
Honcho ES
Nippon Yusen Navigation Museum
Iseyama Kotai Jingu Shrine
Miyazakicho
Yokohama Island Tower
Bashamichi
ZONOHANA PARK
Shiju Kaikan Public Hall
Yokohama Sakuragi
Honcho
Kaigan-dori
Osambashi Kokusai Kyakusen Terminal
Bigiwai-za Theater
Gyoza-no Ohsho
Kanagawa Prefectural Museum of Cultural History
Suigyodo
Benten-bashi Bridge
Toyoko Inn
Yokohama Customs Office
Nogeyama Fudoson
Hanasakicho
Marutani
Ota Machi
Motohamacho
Yokohamasuijo Police Station
Keihin Kyuko Line
Shokuhinkan Aoba
Breeze
Heiwa Plaza
Route Inn Bashamichi
Honcho-dori
Port Opening Square
Downbeat Bay
Onoecho-dori
Legend
Hiyoshi Bldg
Bentendori
Minatomirai Line
Kanagawa Prefectural Office
Yokohama Archives of History
Rest House
Mandarin
Noge Chiku Center
Basil
Nogecho
Basha-michi
Autocom Japan Inc.
Minaminaka-dori
Oimatsu Jr. HS
Richmond
Otamachi
Silk Center & Museum
Akaikutsu Haiteta Onnanoko Statue
YAMASHITA PIER
Yokohama City Chuo Library
Kamome
Kannai Hall
Minaminakadori
Metropolitan
Takiwacho
Comfort Kannai
Benten-dori
Port Opening Memorial Hall
Nippon-odori
Yokohama-Minato Continental
Hikawa Maru Ocean Liner
Miyagawacho
Onoecho
Yoshidamachi
Marinard Underground Shopping Mall
Drug Store
Apa-Kannai
Kannaisakura-dori
Aioicho
Toyoko Inn
Center for Int'l Commerce and Industry
Kanagawa Kenmin Hall (Civic Hall)
Fountain "Goddes of Waters"
Shin-Yamash
Seishonen Koryu Center
Keikyu Store
Gusto
Fukutomicho
Fukutomicho
Kannai
Kannai O-dori
Irifune-dori
Bank of Japan
Nihon-Odori
Mizumachi-dori
Yamashita-koen-dori
Girl Scout Monument
Oimatsu
Hinodecho
Nishidori
Higashidori
Curry Museum
Masagocho
Kannaisaka-dori
Baikotei
Japan Newspaper Museum
Urban History Museum
Yamashita-koen Terminal
Fukutomicho
Isezaki Mall
Minato-Odori
Nihon-Odori
Monterey
Toda Peace Mem. Hall
Three F
Nakadori
Yurin-do Bookshop
Ohana Shoten
Naka Ward Office
Jal City
Minatomirai Line
Yamashita Park
Ikuaikai Clinic
Yokohama Town
Mohan
Yokohama Chuo YMCA
YOKOHAMA PARK
Kaiko-michi
Heichinro Honten
Silk-dori
New Grand
Meidi-Ya
Star
McDonalds
Yokohama Marine Tower
zumagaoka
Chojamachi
Apaiser
Suehirocho
Kannai
Super Kannai
Rose
Sekai-no-Hiroba
Yokohama-eki Negishi dori
Yokohama City Hall
Yokohama Stadium
North Gate
Kagacho Police Station
East Gate
Kanton-dori
Motomachi-Chukagai
Maruetsu Petit
Ne Shrine
Minatocho
Osambashi-dori
NTT
Mielparque
Yokohama Doll Museum
zuma ES
Pachinko
Goraku Wakusei Concorde
Isezakicho
Itsikushima Shrine
Toyoko Inn
Zenrin-mon Gate
Chukagai-Odori
Shanhai-ro
China Town 80
Barneys New York
Yokohama Joint Government Office Building
Metropolitan E'way K1 Yokohama Route
Metropolitan E'way K3 Kariba Route
Hinodecho
Tenya
Horaicho
Grand States
Teisan Kannai
Yoshimoto Aquarium
Chinatown
Daisekai
Hirato Sakuragi
Wakabacho
Bandaicho
Yokohamakoen
Yokohama Garden
JR Negishi Line
Nishimon-dori
Ryusen
Kanteibyo-dori
Hagoromocho
Fureai Yokohama Hospital
Wing Int'l
Windjammer Bar
Kantei-Byo Shrine
Chuzan-ro
Ichiba-dori
Yamasitacho
Yoshinoya
Washington
ODORI PARK
Sukiya
OGMACHI PARK
Minatosogo HS
South Gate
French Hill
Sueyoshicho
7Eleven
Furocho
Hatsunecho
Livemax
Isezakicho-jamachi
HINODEGAWA PARK
Okinacho
West Gate
Yokohama Central Hospital
Motomachi Plaza
Shin-Yamashita
Yayoicho
Yokosuka Kaido
Koganecho
Weekly Mansion
Yokohama Cultural Gymnasium
Yokohama Family Court
Motomachi
Harbor View Park (Minato No Mieru Oka Koen)
Ogicho
Gaikokujin Cemetery
Motomachi Shopping Area
Akebonocho
Municipal Subway Line
Isezaki Police Station
Fujimicho
Yokohama Weekly Mansion, Kannai 3
Kotobukicho
Ishikawacho
Park Square Yokohama
Nakamura River
Iwasaki Museum
British House
Osaragi Memorial Museum
Matsukagecho
Zen
Yamate Jyuban-kan
Kanagawa Museum of Modern Literature
Ishikawacho
to Fujisawa
to Fujisawa
Yamate Museum

who was killed on the Tokaido road in September 1862 by men loyal to Lord Satsuma, an event that sparked the Anglo-Satsuma War of 1863. More recently, there are also servicemen who lost their lives in World War I buried here.

Back on the waterfront, west of Chinatown, the man-made Shinko Island is a mix of Yokohama's present and past, the obvious modern-day element being the 107.5-meter-high Cosmo Clock 21 Ferris wheel, once the largest Ferris wheel in the world, which casts a neon reflection onto the bay at night. The past is the Akarenga (lit. red brick), two long, low red brick warehouses built in 1911 that have been renovated to create a chic waterfront entertainment, shopping and dining complex. All very different to the Yokohama Commodore Perry would have first seen through his spyglass.

RIGHT Heading a few kilometers southward from Yokohama's main central attractions is the fantastic Sankei-en Garden. Opened by businessman Sankei Hara in 1906, the sprawling 175,000-square meter garden is an excellent example of traditional landscaping, combining ponds, streams, lush foliage and striking seasonal colors, meandering trails, and 10 buildings registered as Important Cultural Properties, like the teahouse pictured, that have been brought in from around the country.

LEFT Nearly 10 kilometers south of Yokohama Station and the main bayside area, Hakkejima Sea Paradise is home to one of Japan's best aquariums, with more than 500 species of fish on display. The complex also has white-knuckle rides, a shopping mall and a hotel.

ABOVE Merchants sell grilled fish at Yokohama's fish market. **LEFT** The beach at Umino Park in southern Yokohama. In the background is Hakkejima Sea Paradise's roller coaster, which swings out over the ocean, and its Blue Fall attraction, which thrills, or terrorizes, with a stomach-churning 107-meter vertical drop.

KAMAKURA

In mid-September every year, Tsurugaoka Hachiman-gu Shrine in Kamakura turns back the clock to the area's glory days as the samurai costume parades and horseback archery displays of the shrine's Reitaisai Festival offer a weekend-long glimpse of Kamakura when, from 1192 to 1333, the town was the cultural, political and spiritual center of Japan.

Kamakura's period of prominence began after the Genpei War of 1180–5, during which the Minamoto clan defeated the Taira clan (and some factions within the Minamoto clan itself!) and shortly after established themselves under leader Yoritomo Minamoto in Kamakura as Japan's ruling family. In the 140 years of the Kamakura era that followed, they created an incredibly rich legacy that is still very visible in modern Kamakura.

That legacy is nowhere more striking than in Hase, several stations away from Kamakura on the trundling Enoshima Electric Railway, where the 13.35-meter-tall Daibutsu (Great Statue of Buddha) has held court on its stone pedestal at Kotoku-in Temple for the last 750 years, sitting crossed-legged, eyes closed in meditation and with a smile of contentment on his face that is almost as enigmatic as the Mona Lisa's. Although the Daibutsu has lost the great hall that once housed him (washed away in a tsunami in 1495), and his bronze finish, which some historians speculate might have originally been covered in gold leaf, is now a well-worn mixture of gray, green and soft metallic blue, he has nevertheless managed to come through numerous natural and man-made disasters in amazingly good condition.

Back in Kamakura proper are another 85 historic temples and shrines that reflect the importance of both Buddhism and Shintoism, Japan's indigenous religion, in Kamakura's heyday. For the latter, there is no more magnificent example than the majestic Tsurugaoka Hachiman-gu, entered through a towering, vermilion lacquered *torii* gateway, shortly after which come a series of small humpback bridges that take visitors past two ponds, the Heike and Gempei, supposedly designed by the wife of Yoritomo Minamoto. Both speak of the violence and brutality that marked the Kamakura era, the four islands in the Heike pond symbolizing the death of the Minamoto's enemies (the Japanese for "four" sounds like the word for "death") and the three islands in the Gempei pond inspired by the Chinese character for birth and representing Minamoto's victory over the Taira.

As for Buddhism, there are few temples of greater importance than Kencho-ji, the head temple of the Rinzai sect of Buddhism and Japan's oldest Zen training monastery. Although none of the current structures here date to Kencho-ji's foundation in 1253 or to the peak of its

LEFT The 750-year-old Daibutsu (Great Buddha) at Kotoku-in Temple is the Kamakura area's main draw. The copper statue, which depicts the Amida Buddha, weighs in at an estimated 120 tons and, pedestal included, is just over 13 meters tall. Style-wise, it is said to be typical of Kamakura-era Buddhist sculpture even though the exact designer is unknown.

FAR LEFT Tsurugaoka Hachiman-gu, Kamakura's most important shrine, is steeped in history. It is also the site of the Reitaisai, one of the Kanto region's most impressive historic parades and festivals.

BELOW An ancient bamboo forest in Kamakura. One of Kamakura's distinctive features is the way in which the area's temples and shrines blend with and are accented by nature, be that autumnal colors or the pink and white hues of cherry blossoms in spring.

Kamakura
500 m
1000 ft
Scale 1 : 30,000
N
Eiko Gakuen Jr.HS & HS
Toshiba Design Center
Shiseido Kamakura Factory
Iwase
Sakaeseijinkae Hospital
Kuden ES
Katsuradainaka
Kaminocho
Oh! Plaza
Ito Yokoda
Katsuradain ishi
Katsuradaihi gashi
Yokohama Kamigo Post Office
Ueki HS
Ofuna
Dila
OFUNA
Lumine
Kamakura Women's University
7 Eleven
Sainen-ji
Katsuradaim inami
Inoyamacho
Ofuna Kannon-ji
Kamakura Performing Art Center
Kudencho
Tamanawa kindergarten
Kamakura Okamoto Post Office
Ofuna Central Hospital
Katsuradai ES
Ofuna ES
Familymart
Tamanawa ES
Create
Tamanawa Library
Tamanawa Jr.HS
Konan Ofuna
Mitsubishi Electric
Okamoto
Dai
Iwase Jr. HS
Ofuna Botanical Garden
Denka
Ofuna Jr. HS
Noshi
Hakusan Shrine
Kita-Kamakura Museum
Ofuna HS
Imaizumi ES
Fujimicho
Fuji
Create
Tamon-in
JR. Tokaido Line
Kobukuroya
Osaka ES
Imaizumi
Kamakura CC
Yamazaki
Kamakuradai Post Office
Takano
Kohachi Shrine
Sanzaigaike Shinrin Park
Mitsubishi Electric
HANA Guest House Kamakura
Villa Kita Kamakura
Shozoku-in
Kamakura Kosaka Post Office
Kita Kamakura
Imaizumidai
Kamimachiya
Shonan Machiya
Yamasaki Elementary School
Engaku-ji
Yamanouchi
Kamakura Old Pottery Museum
Fujitsuka ES
Kita Kamakura Joshi Gakuen
Toshimaya
Meigetsuyo
Tokei-ji
Fuka
Grave of Hojo Tokiyori
JR EAST KAMAKURA TRAIN BASE
Terabun
Matsu-ga-oka Bunko
Hachinoki
Tachibana
Kencho-ji Hanso-bo
Yo Shomei Museum
Meigetsu-in
KAMAKURA CENTRAL PARK
Jochi-ji
Kamakura Gozan
Tengen-in
Tokiwa
Shonan Fukasawa
Kencho-ji Zen
Kaishun-in
Kyoraian
Fukasawa ES
Choju-ji
Dokei-in
Nishimikado
Kajiwara
Kamakura Gakuen HS
Kakuon-ji
Binya Coffee
Fukasawa Jr. HS
Kamakura Kajiwara Post Office
Hachinoki
Shonan Monorail
Enno-ji
Grave of Yoritomo
Grave of Hino Toshimoto
Kaizo-ji
Pref. Modern Art Museum Kamakura Annex
JR Yokosuka Line
Daisho Kangiten
Raiko-ji
Yakuo-ji
Yagumo Shrine
Zuisen-ji
Shonan Memorial Hospital
Kuzuharagaoka Shrine
Myoden-ji
Tsurugaoka Hachiman-gu Shrine
Egara Tenjin Shrine
Kamakura-gu Shrine
GENJIYAMA PARK
Jokomyo-ji
Fueda
The Museum of Modern Art, Kamakura & Hayama
Nikaido
Hojo-shi Tokiwa-tei site
Kamakura Museum of National Treasures
Grave of Hojo Masako
Sasuke Inari Shrine
Zeniarai Benten Shrine
Yukinoshita
Yabusame -baba
Jufuku-ji
Mikawaya
Daini ES
Jomyo-ji
DAIBUTSUZAKA HIKING COURSE
FUEDA PARK
Yagumo Shrine
Enkyu-ji
Kaburagi Kiyokata Memorial Art Museum
Azumaya
Beniya
Hokai-ji
Sugimoto-dera
Minowa
Tatsumi Shrine
Tsurugaoka Kaikan
Kiyokawa Hospital
Kamakura Jomyo-ji Post Office
Ogigayatsu
Komori Shrine
Daibutsu Kiritoshi
Fukudori
Wakamiya Oji
Kamakurabori Kaikan
Daini Jr.HS
Junis
Sengen Shrine
Kinokuniya
Kitchoan Museum
Hokkoku-ji
Suwa Shrine
Kamakura Mori
Myoryu-ji
Sasuke
Kamakura City Hall
KAMAKURA
Rinkan Hospital
Daibutsu (The Great Buddha of Hase)
Kamakura Otani Memorial Art Museum
Onari ES
Kamakura
Daigyo-ji
Ruin of the Residence of Hojo Tokimasa
Hongakuji-ji
Myohon-ji
Tanigoro
Onarimachi
Munakata Print Museum
Kotoku-in
Sotatsu
Izumi
Komachien
Omachi
Joei-ji
Toshimaya
Sankaido
Amanawa Shrine
Kamakura Museum of Literature
Yagumo Shrine
Daiho-ji
Gokuraku-ji
Kaseiro
Yuigahama
Hyakuen
Yohira
Sasamemachi
Okuni
An-yo-ji
Motokids
Kosoku-ji
Ishibashi
HASE
Yuigahama
Kamakura Gymnasium
Kamakura Jogakuin HS
Jogyo-ji
Takenoya
Kamakura Kindergarten
Kamakura Orgoldo
Wadazuka
Mita Memorial Gymnasium
Honko-ji
Myoho-ji
Hase-dera
Rental Cycle
Enoshima Line
Sea Front
Nukada Memorial Hospital
Jashumon
Denny's
Goryo Shrine
Hase
Kaihinso Kamakura
Yuigahama
Kamakura Minor Court
Ankokuron-ji
HISAGI OI PARK
Kamakura Sichirigahama Post Office
Inamuragasaki ES
Hase YH
KKR Kamakura Wakamiya
Keiun-ji
JR Yokosuka Line
Gokuraku-ji
Myocho-ji
Zushi Highland Post Office
Gokurakuji
Chikaramochiya
Kamakura Municipal Inasegawa Nursery School
Kofuku-ji
Chosho-ji
Myoko-ji
Sichirigahamahigashi
Sakanoshita
Toraji
Raiko-ji
Joju-in
Sarah
Gosho Shrine
Gokurakuji
Ajisaiso
Yuigahama
Zaimokuza
Kuhon-ji
Hossho-ji
Zaimokuza
Kamakura Prince
Kamakura Park
Komyo-ji
Fudaraku-ji
Ganden-ji
Banquet Hall Shichirigahama
Inamuragasaki
Sagami Bay
Hisagi
Endoden Line
7 Eleven
Hisagi ES
Sichirigahama
KAMAKURA KAIHIN PARK
Kotsubo
Myoko-ji

ABOVE The more than 110-year-old Enoshima Electric Railway, or Enoden, runs a 10-kilometer single-track route from Kamakura to Fujisawa, stopping among other places at Hase, making the trundling two-carriage units the most common way of getting to the Daibutsu.
LEFT From mid-June to early July, 2,000 plus hydrangea enshroud the stairway leading to the main building at Joju-in Temple, from where visitors get some of the best views over Kamakura.

LEFT A round window frames the view of the garden at Meigetsu-in Temple.
RIGHT Before entering the grounds of a shrine, it is tradition to purify oneself by rinsing one's hands and mouth. First, use the ladle at the purification fountain to pour water over your hands. Then pour more water into a cupped hand, which you use to rinse your mouth before spitting it out by (not in!) the fountain. Not many people actually do the mouth rinse nowadays, but if you do, be aware that it is bad manners to sip directly from the ladle.

of its powers when it could boast 49 subtemples, the mix of Chinese and Japanese architectural styles is still impressive. Another gem is Tokei-ji, founded in the 13th century as a nunnery that became known as a place of refuge for abused wives. Sometimes overlooked by visitors in favor of more well-known temples, Tokei-ji's grounds are transformed seasonally, by irises in June, bush clover in September, apricot blossom in February and magnolia in March, a perfect example of how traditional Japanese design and sensibilities are interwoven with natural appreciation.

HAKONE AND MOUNT FUJI

There is something almost hypnotic about Mount Fuji, a combination of aesthetics and scale that has worked the mountain deep into the Japanese psyche. At 3,776 meters, the near perfectly symmetrical Fuji-san, as the mountain is known in Japanese, is Japan's tallest peak, her feet planted in the prefectures of both Yamanashi and Shizuoka where she looms large above all else from all parts, even as far away as central Tokyo on clear days.

With her presence felt far and wide, it is no wonder Fuji-san has had a lasting cultural and spiritual influence on Japan. The country's most famous *ukiyo-e* (woodblock print) printmaker, Katsuhika Hokusai (1760–1849), was so awed by the peak that much of his life was spent capturing her various guises, his most notable depiction being the now iconic "Great Wave Off Kanagawa" from his series *36 Views of Mount Fuji,* in which a snow-capped Fuji is seen far off in the distance as a giant foaming wave is set to break violently in the foreground.

Religions have been similarly influenced, Fuji long having been considered a sacred site and a place of pilgrimage. In Buddhism, Fuji-san is home to Dainichi Nyorai, the Buddha of All-Illuminating Wisdom, while in Shintoism, the indigenous religion of Japan,

ABOVE Climbers skirt the crater near the summit of Mount Fuji. Based on current seismic activity in the area, some experts believe the dormant volcano has the potential to erupt in the relatively near future, but that does not put off the thousands upon thousands of hikers who make the arduous trek to its peak every summer.
BELOW The cable car that carries visitors over the steaming vents of the Owakudani Valley.

Fuji-san is the home of a fire god and a goddess of trees, the former not so farfetched for a dormant volcano, although the latter is harder to fathom given how bare the mountain is.

Although in the annual July–August climbing season some 250,000 people make the six- to eight-hour trek up barren trails to Fuji's peak, for the majority of Tokyoites an up-close trip to Fuji-san means a weekend in Hakone, roughly 100 kilometers west of central Tokyo, to enjoy the area's natural hot springs, traditional inns (*ryokan*) and stunning mountain and lakeside scenery.

It is a break that follows a very well-beaten route, taking in an unusually diverse range of transportation that starts from Hakone-Yumoto Station with a ride on the two-carriage Hakone-Tozan switchback railway, which slowly weaves upward through a succession of one-platform stations to the mountain village of Gora. Here, sight-seers switch to a funicular train that takes them up to the 800-meter

ABOVE The classic postcard view of Hakone and Mount Fuji gatecrashed by one of the mock galleons that take tourists on trips out on Lake Ashi.
OPPOSITE Fuji-san and the Chureito Pagoda at Arakura Sengen Shrine in Fujiyoshida, Yamanashi Prefecture. Since the pagoda was built in the 1960s, the shrine has become a popular place for photo-graphing Fuji, especially in the fall. Other classic view-points include Fuji-san set behind the lush green tea fields of Shizuoka Prefecture.

Hakone & Mt Fuji
5 km
2 miles
Scale 1 : 200 000
N
FUEFUKI CITY
OTSUKI CITY
UENOHARA
FUJIKAWAGUCHIKO TOWN
NISHIKATSURA TOWN
TSURU CITY
DOSHI VILLAGE
FUJIYOSHIDA CITY
NARUSAWA VILLAGE
OSHINO VILLAGE
YAMANAKAKO VILLAGE
YAMAKITA
FUJI-HAKONE-IZU NATIONAL PARK
OYAMA TOWN
GOTEMBA CITY
MINAMIASHIGARA
FUJINOMIYA CITY
HAKONE
SUSONO CITY
FUJI CITY
NUMAZU TOWN
NAGAIZUMI TOWN
YUGAWARA
KEISEI
Chuo E'way
JR Chuo Line
Misaka-michi
Kamikurokoma Bypass
Mt Shakagatake
Mt Kuro-dake
Mt Mitsutoge
Kaiseido Hospital
City Hospital
Otsuki Garden Golf Course
Akiyama Country Club
Mt Akakuraga-take
Miyako Golf Course
Tsuru University
Tsurubunka University
Fujikyu Otsuki Line
Mt Settogatake
Mt Kanayama
Mt Kenashi
O-dake 1623m
Lake Kawaguchi
Fuji Viewing Platform
Lake Saiko
Kawaguchiko
Fujikawaguchiko Town Office
Fuji Yoshida Michael's American Pub
Eboshi-san Lookout
Koyo-dai Lookout
Fugaku Wind Cave
Narusawa Ice Cave
Aokigahara Ocean of Trees
Fuji Panorama Line
Kawaguchiko GC
Sengen Shrine
City Hospital
Oshino-hakkai Springs
Health Science University
Fujizakura Country Club
Fuji Kawaguchiko Golf Course
Motosu-fuketsu
Fuji Fuketsu Air Hole
Mt Omuro 1468m
Fuji Lakeside Country Club
Higashi - Fuji Goko Rd
Mt Mishotai 1682m
Mt Omuro
Mt Komotsurushi
Hinokibora Maru
Mt Ishiwari 1413m
Mt Ohira
Doushi Rd
Lake Yamanaka
Marino-dori
Mt Mikuni
Mt Obora
Miho Dam
Mt Furo
Mt Takamatsu
Asagiri Country Club
Fuji Chuo Golf Course
Kawaguchi-ko Route
Mt Fuji Toll Rd
Kawaguchi-ko Yoshida-guchi 5th Station
Yoshidaguchi Route
Nakanochaya
Nyonin Tenjo
Self Defense Force
Komitake Shrine
Omuro Sengen Shrine
Komitake Shrine
Mt Fuji 3776m
Subashiri Route
Subashiri New 5th Station
Fuji-kogen Golf Course
Sengen Shrine
Taiyo Golf Course
Fuji Oyama Golf Course
Higashi Fuji Golf Course
Fuji Green Hill Golf Course
Check Mate CC
Tomei E'way
Surugaoyama
Gotemba Line
Hoei-san 2693m
Fujinomiya/ Mishima 5th Station
Gotemba 5th Station
Komitake Shrine
Fuji-heigen Golf Course
Fuji-kokusai Golf Course
Hakoneura H'way
Gotemba Route
Mt Fuji Skyline
The National Golf Course
JSDF FIELD
Gotembakogen Hospital
Tobu Hospital
Mt Yagura-dake
Izu Hakone Railway Daiyuzan Line
Daiyuzan
Daiyuzan Saijo-ji
Shiraito-no-taki Waterfall
Fujinomiya / Mishima Route
Mt Fuji Skyline
Nippon Land How Amusement Parks
Gotemba
Taiheiyo Golf Course
Jinbayama Shrine
Mt Kintoki
Mt Myojinga-dake
Odawara Flower Garden
Lalique Museum, Hakone
Venetian Glass Museum
Hakone Botanical Garden of Wetlands
Suwa Shrine
Tsujimura Botanical Park
Dogashima Hot Spring
Basho-in
Fuji Safari Park
Mt Fuji Children's World
Minamifuji Hospital
Mt Kurodake
Tomei E'way
Gotemba Line
Hakone Skyline
Gotenba GC
Hakone Ropeway
Owakudani
Kowakidani Hot Spring
Gora
Hakone Tozan Railway
Echizen-ga-take 1507m
Koyamafukusei Hospital
Mt Kamiyama
Chisuji-no-taki Waterfall
Hakone Garden Museum
Sangen Shrine
Shinfuji Hospital
Fujinomiya
Minobu Line
Ofuji Hospital
Seimei Hospital
Mt Otake
Iwanami
Tomeisusono Hospital
Hakone-en Garden
Ashinoko Skyline
Lake Ashinoko
Toyo Tires Turnpike
Tokaido Shinkansen
Takaoka Hospital
Nishi-Fuji Rd
Fuji Tokoha University
Mt Ashitaka 1187m
Seisuikan Hospital
Hakone Barrier Museum
Odawarajo CC
Mt Myojo
Tomei E'way
Bamboo Botanical Garden
Ashinoko CC
Daikanzen

LEFT Hakone is well known for *onsen* (hot spring baths) like this very traditional and typical *rotemburo* (outdoor bath), where besides providing a wonderful place to unwind, the mineral-rich waters are said to alleviate numerous ailments.

BELOW LEFT One of the sculptures at the Hakone Open Air Museum. A very popular detour on the classic Hakone sightseeing route, the OAM has 100 pieces spread across its grounds in addition to a 300-piece Picasso collection.

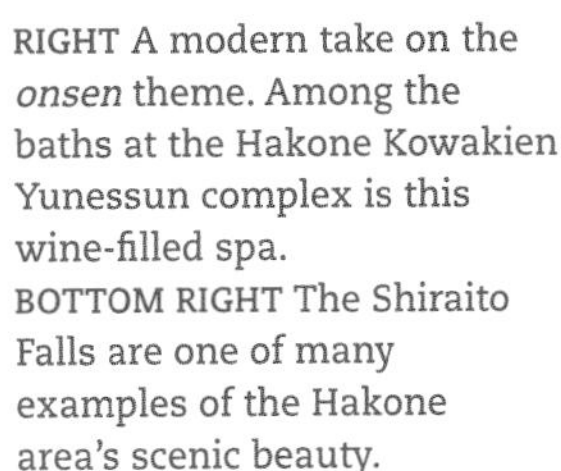

RIGHT A modern take on the *onsen* theme. Among the baths at the Hakone Kowakien Yunessun complex is this wine-filled spa.

BOTTOM RIGHT The Shiraito Falls are one of many examples of the Hakone area's scenic beauty.

Mount Soun (Sounzan), where they then hop aboard a cable car that carries them over the steaming volcanic valley of Owakudani (aptly meaning "Great Boiling Valley").

It is not quite Dante's vision of hell, but the bare landscape, punctuated by gently bubbling hot spring pools and sulfur vents that ooze steam, would not look out of place in Mordor. The cable car then works its way down from the mountains, terminating at Lake Ashi (Ashi-no-ko), where a large part of the tourist horde heads straight onto one of the mock pirate galleons that cruise the lake, while others wait for the boats to get out of shot so they can snap the postcard view of Hakone, a snow-capped Mount Fuji looming large behind the lake, the verdant rim of which is accented by the giant vermilion *torii* gateway of Hakone Shrine.

NIKKO

Nikko, 120 kilometers north of Tokyo in the rural surrounds of Tochigi Prefecture, provides a tranquil natural setting for an Edo-era architectural masterpiece, the Tosho-gu Shrine complex built to enshrine Tokugawa Ieyasu, the first of the Edo-era shoguns.

There are few buildings in Japan as extravagant in their design. The shrine's Yomei-mon (aptly meaning Sun Blaze Gate), a roofed gateway standing 11 meters in height, is an almost garish blend of black, gold, red and green accented by more than 500 ornately carved dancing maidens, birds, dragons and flowers, while the less lavish white and gold of the nearby Kara-mon Gate provides the backdrop for more elaborate carvings that are said to depict Chinese legends. Then there is the deep red five-story pagoda, frustratingly positioned for modern-day visitors to be nigh on impossible to fully capture top to bottom in a photograph, which, like the gateways, is adorned with hundreds of intricate decorations. It is not hard to see why it took 15,000 craftsmen almost two years to construct the Tosho-gu complex, in the process going through an estimated 2.5 million sheets of gold leaf.

OPPOSITE LEFT The Shinkyo Bashi bridge was once reserved for use by *daimyo* and their entourages as they traveled to Tosho-gu Shrine.
OPPOSITE RIGHT One of the guardians that sits within the Yomei-mon Gate at Tosho-gu.
ABOVE A small part of the Tosho-gu complex, with the Yomei-mon Gate in the background.
RIGHT The Yayoi Festival, which heralds the arrival of spring with a parade of 12 ornately decorated floats, has been held in Nikko since the 8th century.

ABOVE The original three wise monkeys at Tosho-gu. "Hear no evil, Speak no evil, See no evil" is a key principle of Tendai Buddhism.

Besides the architecture, a walk around Tosho-gu brings several more understated points of interest. Hanging above the shrine's sacred stables is a famous carving of the three wise monkeys, a representation of the three main principles of Tendai Buddhism (the origin of "Hear no evil, Speak no evil, See no evil"). Shortly after that, on the way to Ieyasu's unexpectedly plain tomb, is the Nemuri Neko carving of a sleeping cat, dating to either the 16th or 17th century and sometimes attributed to a possibly fictitious Edo-era sculptor called Hidari Jingoro. After the initial shock and awe brought on by Tosho-gu's colorful assault on the senses, it is these small details and the hundreds of other miniature reliefs and carvings that bring on a more lasting appreciation of the craftsmanship that went into Ieyasu's resting place.

LEFT An example of the color found throughout Tosho-gu.

Near Tosho-gu are several other structures of note that combine with Ieyasu's shrine to form a grand Edo statement of wealth and power. A few minutes to the south, the Tendai sect's Rinno-ji Temple complex features a main hall, the Sanbutsudo, that houses three giant gilded Buddha and Kannon statues, while a little further south of that is the Shinkyo Bashi, a small but striking vermilion footbridge once for the exclusive use of *daimyo* and their entourages to cross the foaming Daiya River on their way to Tosho-gu. Completing the three main religious complexes in the area is Futarasan Shrine, to which Shinkyo Bashi belongs, a short walk west of Tosho-gu. Far less colorful and grand in its design, it is home to dozens of National Treasures.

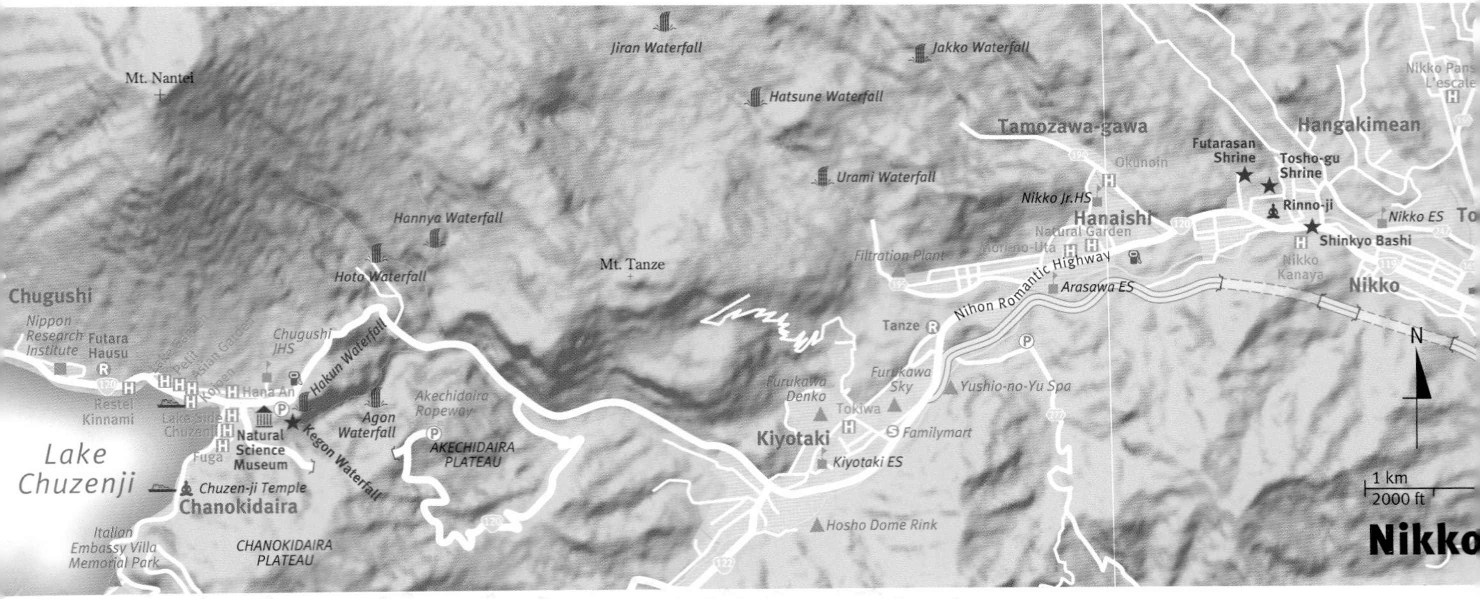

Nikko
Mt. Nantei
Jiran Waterfall
Jakko Waterfall
Hatsune Waterfall
Urami Waterfall
Hannya Waterfall
Hoto Waterfall
Mt. Tanze
Tamozawa-gawa
Hangakimean
Futarasan Shrine
Tosho-gu Shrine
Rinno-ji
Shinkyo Bashi
Nikko ES
Nikko Jr.HS
Hanaishi
Natural Garden
Filtration Plant
Nihon Romantic Highway
Arasawa ES
Nikko Kanaya
Nikko
Tanze
Chugushi
Nippon Research Institute
Futara Hausu
Chugushi JHS
Hakun Waterfall
Hana An
Restel Kinnami
Lake Side Chuzenji
Natural Science Museum
Kegon Waterfall
Agon Waterfall
Akechidaira Ropeway
AKECHIDAIRA PLATEAU
Furukawa Denko
Furukawa Sky
Tokiwa
Yushio-no-Yu Spa
Kiyotaki
Familymart
Kiyotaki ES
Lake Chuzenji
Fuga
Chuzen-ji Temple
Chanokidaira
Italian Embassy Villa Memorial Park
CHANOKIDAIRA PLATEAU
Hosho Dome Rink
N
1 km
2000 ft

LEFT Lots of day trippers to Nikko tend to visit only Tosho-gu Shrine and its immediate neighbors, but with an overnight stay you can also take in Nikko's wonderful natural surrounds at sights like the pictured Lake Chuzenji and Kegon Falls.

BELOW With red bibs and often red hats, Jizo statues are a common sight in Japan. They are said to guide travelers in the real and spiritual worlds, and in particular dead children.
BOTTOM Shinto priests climb one of the stairways at Tosho-gu. Many of the rocks and statues in and around Tosho-gu have been partially reclaimed by moss, helping to give the site a wonderfully ancient feel.

PHOTO CREDITS

All photos © Rob Goss, except the following:
Front cover MivPiv/istockphoto.com; Sean Pavone/Shutterstock.com; Pichung/Dreamstime.com; anouchka/istockphoto.com; Sira Anamwong/Shutterstock.com; Club4traveler/Shutterstock.com; Tupungato/Shutterstock.com; vichie81/Shutterstock.com; RAYphotographer/Shutterstock.com; Amy Nichole Harris/Shutterstock.com; Ralph Paprzycki/Dreamstime.com; Tooykrub/Shutterstock.com
Front flap TommL/istockphoto.com
Spine Sakarin Sawasdinaka/Shutterstock.com
Back cover Capelson/Dreamstime.com; joel-t/istockphoto.com; EdStock/istockphoto.com; Santanor/Dreamstime.com; JNTO; aluxum/istockphoto.com; Sean Pavone/Dreamstime.com; Mike K./Dreamstime.com;
Front endpapers Sean Pavone/Dreamstime.com
Back endpapers jaimax/istockphoto.com
1 fotoVoyager/istockphoto.com
2/3 Simone Matteo Giuseppe Manzoni/Dreamstime.com
4 (left) lechatnoir/istockphoto.com; **4 (middle)** JNTO; **4 (right)** skyearth/Shutterstock.com
5 (left) Xiye/Dreamstime.com;
6/7 Rawpixel/istockphoto.com
9 (far left) JNTO; **9 (2nd from left)** Ybaechtold/Dreamstime.com; **9 (middle)** Sean Pavone/Dreamstime.com; **9 (2nd from right)** Apichart Wannawal/Dreamstime.com; **9 (far right)** anouchka/istockphoto.com
10 (top) Attila JANDI/Shutterstock.com;
10/11 (bottom left) aluxum/istockphoto.com
11 (top left) EdStock/istockphoto.com;
11 (middle right) aluxum/istockphoto.com;
11 (bottom right) MivPiv/istockphoto.com;
12 (top left) Sakuragirin/Dreamstime.com;
12 (top right) Pal Teravagimov/Shutterstock.com;
12 (middle) Sean Pavone/Dreamstime.com;
12 (bottom left) RAYphotographer/Shutterstock.com; **12 (bottom right)** JNTO
13 (top) aluxum/istockphoto.com; **13 (middle)** Hannamariah/Shutterstock.com; **13 (bottom)** Sean Pavone/Shutterstock.com
14 (left) Yasufumi Nishi/JNTO; **14 (right)** JNTO
15 (top) aluxum/istockphoto.com; **15 (bottom left)** Attila JANDI/Shutterstock.com; **15 (bottom right)** Christian Baumle/Dreamstime.com
16 (left) Yasufumi Nishi/JNTO; **16 (top left)** BernardAllum/istockphoto.com; **16 (top right)** BernardAllum/istockphoto.com; **16 (bottom)** Wdeon/Dreamstime.com
17 (top left) Ronald Sumners/Shutterstock.com;
17 (top right) BernardAllum/istockphoto.com;
17 (middle) JNTO; **17 (bottom)** 000zzz/Dreamstime.com
18 (left) Aaa187/Dreamstime.com
18/19 (bottom middle) JNTO
19 (top) woojpn/istockphoto.com; 1**9 (bottom right)** J. Henning Buchholz/Dreamstime.com
20 (top left) Tochigi Prefectural Tourism Association Tokyo Office/JNTO; **20 (middle)** hakkaisan/istockphoto.com
20/21 Attila JANDI/Shutterstock.com
21 (top right) cowardlion/Shutterstock.com; **21 (bottom left)** sack/istockphoto.com; **21 (bottom right)** Willy Setiadi/Dreamstime.com
22 (bottom) sack/istockphoto.com
23 (middle) Sakarin Sawasdinaka/Shutterstock.com; **23 (right)** Oblachko/Dreamstime.com; **23 (left)** Zhiqiang Hu/Dreamstime.com
24 (top right) kana/photolibrary.jpn; **24 (middle)** woojpn/istockphoto.com; **24 (bottom)** lechatnoir/istockphoto.com
24/25 (top middle) befa/istockphoto.com; **24/25 (bottom middle)** Balipapa/photolibrary.jpn
25 (top right) siraanamwong/istockphoto.com;
25 (bottom right) Siraanamwong/ Dreamstime.com
26 (left) EdStock/istockphoto.com; **26 (right)** aluxum/istockphoto.com
27 (top) aluxum/istockphoto.com; **27 (middle)** TayaCho/istockphoto.com; **27 (bottom)** Angela Ostafichuk/ Dreamstime.com
28 (top left) monocrom-studio/istockphoto.com;
28 (bottom) JNTO
28/29 (top middle) Sean Pavone/Dreamstime.com
29 (top right) photoclicks/istockphoto.com; **29 (bottom)** aluxum/istockphoto.com
30 (left) amasann/photolibrary.jpn; **30 (right)** ギトシコユルギ/photolibrary.jpn
31 (top left) Apichart Wannawal/Dreamstime.com; **31 (top right)** & **31 (bottom)** aluxum/istockphoto.com;
32 (top) Yuryz/Dreamstime.com; 32 (bottom) Yurix Sardinelly/Dreamstime.com
33 (top) tororo reaction/Shutterstock.com; **33 (middle)**/カモンミール photolibrary.jpn; **33 (bottom and right bottom)** cowardlion/Dreamstime.com; **33 (right top)** Y. Shimizu; **33 (right middle)** urbancow/istockphoto.com
34/35 Sean Pavone/Dreamstime.com
37 (far left) Haveseen Dreamstime.com; **37 (2nd from left)** Lucian Milasan/Dreamstime.com; **37 (2nd from right)** choongmin63/istockphoto.com;
37 (far right) JNTO
38 (bottom left) Sean Pavone/Dreamstime.com;
38 (bottom right) Cowardlion/Dreamstime.com
39 (top left) & **39 (right bottom)** Sean Pavone/Dreamstime.com; **39 (right top)** Gritsana P/Shutterstock.com
40 Santanor/Dreamstime.com
41 (top) Haveseen/Dreamstime.com; **41 (bottom left)** Dmitry Ometsinsky Dreamstime.com; **41 (bottom right)** Meisterphotos/Dreamstime.com
42 (top) Actionwatcher/Dreamstime.com; **42 (bottom)** Nathanphoto/Dreamstime.com
43 (top) moon/photolibrary.jpn; **43 (bottom left)** Jorisvo/Dreamstime.com; **43 (bottom right)** Chee-onn Leong/Dreamstime.com
44 (left) Lucian Milasan/Dreamstime.com;
44 (right) Sira Anamwong/123rf.com
45 (top left and top right) winhorse/istockphoto.com; **45 (bottom)** aluxum/istockphoto.com
46 (top) Aivoges/Dreamstime.com; **46 (bottom)** Tupungato/Dreamstime.com
46/47 (bottom middle) JNTO
47 (top) Steve Allen/Dreamstime.com; **47 (middle)** JNTO; **47 (bottom)** aluxum/istockphoto.com

48 (left) JayTurbo/istockphoto.com; **48 (right)** choongmin63/istockphoto.com
48/49 (bottom) Tifonimages/Dreamstime.com
49 (top left) Paolo Gianti/Shutterstock.com;
49 (top right) Rozenn Leard/Dreamstime.com
50/51 Mike K./Dreamstime.com
53 (far left) Torsakarin/Dreamstime.com;
53 (2nd from left) Sean Pavone/Dreamstime.com; **53 (2nd from right)** a_text/photolibary.jpn;
53 (far right) fishwork/istockphoto.com
54 aluxum/istockphoto.com
54/55 SeanPavone/Dreamstime.com
55 (top) aluxum/istockphoto.com; **55 (middle)** beibaoke/Shutterstock.com; **55 (bottom)** EdStock/istockphoto.com
56 (top) Mihai-bogdan Lazar/Dreamstime.com;
56 (bottom) John Alphonse/Dreamstime.com
57 (top) journey2008/istockphoto.com; **57 (middle)** holgs/istockphoto.com; **57 (bottom left)** Ponsulak/Dreamstime.com; **57 (bottom right)** Mihai-bogdan Lazar/Dreamstime.com
58 Club4traveler/Shutterstock.com
59 (top) Tooykrub/Shutterstock.com; **59 (bottom)** Sean Pavone | Dreamstime.com
60 (top) a_text/photolibary.jpn; **60 (bottom)** moon/photolibrary.jpn
61 (top) takamichi/photolibrary.jpn; **61 (bottom)** TAGSTOCK1/istockphoto.com
62 (top) Thanomphong Jantarotjana/123rf.com;
62 (top left) Mike K./Dreamstime.com;
62 (bottom) Beibaoke1/Dreamstime.com
63 (top right) Cowardlion/Dreamstime.com;
63 (bottom left) Siraanamwong/Dreamstime.com; **63 (bottom right)** fishwork/istockphoto.com
64/65 (top left) Kennethchern/Dreamstime.com
65 (top) わかざる/photolibrary.jpn; **65 (middle and bottom right)** 源/photolibrary.jpn;
65 (bottom left) a_text/photolibary.jpn
66/67 Sean Pavone/Shutterstock.com
69 (far left) tungtopgun/Shutterstock.com;
69 (2nd from left) Law Alan/123rf.com; **69 (2nd from right)** Pornsak Paewlumfaek/Shutterstock.com; **69 (far right)** Aaa187/Dreamstime.com
70 Mlenny/istockphoto.com
70/71 (middle top) Jo Chambers/Shutterstock.com; **70/71 (middle bottom)** Yuryz/Dreamstime.com
71 (top) Law Alan/123rf.com; **71 (bottom right)** mat/photolibrary.jpn
72 (top) Siraanamwong/Dreamstime.com; **72 (bottom)** TOHO/photolibrary.jpn
73 (top) woojpn/istockphoto.com; **73 (bottom)** 仙人 カメ仙人/photolibrary.jpn
74 tungtopgun/Shutterstock.com
75 (top) Sean Pavone/Dreamstime.com;
75 (bottom) hi2-photo/photolibrary.jpn
76 (top) Aaa187/Dreamstime.com; **76 (bottom)** JNTO
77 (top left) Siraanamwong | Dreamstime.com;
77 (top right) Steveng1892/Dreamstime.com;
77 (bottom)みるく/photolibrary.jpn
78 (right) GOTO_TOKYO/istockphoto.com; **78 (left)** Pornsak Paewlumfaek/Shutterstock.com
79 (top) みな/photolibrary.jpn; **79 (bottom left)** Pichung/Dreamstime.com; **79 (bottom right)** Mihai-bogdan Lazar/Dreamstime.com
80/81 Ralph Paprzycki/Dreamstime.com
83 (far left) suchi187/123rf.com; **83 (2nd left)** anouchka/istockphoto.com; **83 (2nd right)** Capelson/Dreamstime.com; **83 (far right)** Mike K./Dreamstime.com
84 (top left) Andrew Holmgren/Dreamstime.com; **84 (top right)** and **85 (top)** Siraanamwong/Dreamstime.com
85 (bottom left) winhorse/istockphoto.com
86 (left) chemc/istockphoto.com; **86 (right top)** Siraanamwong/Dreamstime.com; **86 (right bottom)** aluxum/istockphoto.com
87 (right) greir11/Dreamstime.com
88 (left) Retina2020/Dreamstime.com;
88 (right) Cowardlion/Dreamstime.com
89 (top left) Cowardlion/Dreamstime.com;
89 (top right) aluxum/istockphoto.com; **89 (bottom)** suchi187/123rf.com
90 (top left) anouchka/istockphoto.com; **90 (top right)** Egoeye/Dreamstime.com
90/91 (bottom) Sira Anamwong/Shutterstock.com
91 (top left) Siraanamwong/Dreamstime.com;
91 (top right) anouchka/istockphoto.com
92 (top) aluxum/istockphoto.com; **92 (bottom)** Sean Pavone/Dreamstime.com
93 (top left) Heisenberg85/Dreamstime.com;
93 (top right) Takamex/Shutterstock.com;
93 (bottom left) aluxum/istockphoto.com
94 (bottom) nickfree/istockphoto.com;
94 (top) Farang/Dreamstime.com
94/95 (top) y-studio/istockphoto.com
95 (bottom left) Neale Cousland/Shutterstock.com; **95 (bottom right)** SeanPavonePhoto/istockphoto.com
96 (top) Mike K./Dreamstime.com; **96 (bottom)** fotoVoyager/istockphoto.com
97 (top) tiger_barb/istockphoto.com; **97 (bottom)** Andres Garcia Martin/Dreamstime.com
98/99 TommL/istockphoto.com
101 (far left) skyearth/Shutterstock.com; **101 (2nd left)** Hiro1775/Dreamstime.com; **101 (2nd right)** Aduldej Sukaram/Dreamstime.com;
101 (far right) Sean Pavone/Dreamstime.com
102 (top) repistu/istockphoto.com; **102 (bottom)** JPRichard/Shutterstock.com
103 (top) Akira Okada/JNTO; **103 (bottom left)** joel-t/istockphoto.com; **103 (bottom right)** Mike K./Dreamstime.com
105 (top) Narongsak Nagadhana/Dreamstime.com; **105 (middle)** JNTO; **105 (bottom left)** yama/photolibrary.jpn; **105 (bottom right)** Aduldej Sukaram/Dreamstime.com
106/107 (middle) JNTO
106 (bottom) Hiro1775/Dreamstime.com
107 (right) Malgorzata Gajderowicz/Dreamstime.com
109 (top left) 7maru/istockphoto.com; **109 (top right)** cowardlion/Dreamstime.com; **109 (middle left)** joel-t/istockphoto.com; **109 (bottom right)** cowardlion/Dreamstime.com
110 Sean Pavone/Dreamstime.com
111 (top right) Yuryz/Dreamstime.com; **111 (top left)** skyearth/Shutterstock.com; **111 (bottom)** sack/istockphoto.com
113 (top) Odakyu Electric Railway/JNTO;
113 (middle left) Pcutter/Dreamstime.com;
113 (middle right) EdStock/istockphoto.com;
113 (bottom) Irfan Nurdiansyah/Dreamstime.com
114 (top right) Kessudap/Dreamstime.com;
114 (left) Sean Pavone/Dreamstime.com
115 (top) Sean Pavone/Dreamstime.com;
115 (middle) Tupungato/Dreamstime.com;
115 (bottom right) Tooykrub/Shutterstock.com
116 Yasufumi Nishi/JNTO
117 (left) T.鳥取/photolibrary.jpn; **117 (top right)** beibaoke/Shutterstock.com; **117 (bottom right)** Sean Pavone/Dreamstime.com

Published by Tuttle Publishing, an imprint of Periplus Editions (HK) Ltd

www.tuttlepublishing.com

ISBN: 978-4-8053-1317-6

Distributed by

North America, Latin America & Europe
Tuttle Publishing
364 Innovation Drive
North Clarendon, VT 05759-9436 U.S.A.
Tel: 1 (802) 773-8930; Fax: 1 (802) 773-6993
info@tuttlepublishing.com
www.tuttlepublishing.com

Japan
Tuttle Publishing
Yaekari Building, 3rd Floor
5-4-12 Osaki, Shinagawa-ku
Tokyo 141-0032
Tel: (81) 3 5437-0171;Fax: (81) 3 5437-0755
sales@tuttle.co.jp
www.tuttle.co.jp

Asia Pacific
Berkeley Books Pte. Ltd.
61 Tai Seng Avenue, #02-12; Singapore 534167
Tel: (65) 6280-1330; Fax: (65) 6280-6290
inquiries@periplus.com.sg
www.periplus.com

18 17 16 15   10 9 8 7 6 5 4 3 2 1

Printed in Hong Kong   1503EP

THE TUTTLE STORY

"Books to Span the East and West"

Many people are surprised to learn that the world's leading publisher of books on Asia had humble beginnings in the tiny American state of Vermont. The company's founder, Charles E. Tuttle, belonged to a New England family steeped in publishing.

Tuttle's father was a noted antiquarian book dealer in Rutland, Vermont. Young Charles honed his knowledge of the trade working in the family bookstore, and later in the rare books section of Columbia University Library. His passion for beautiful books—old and new—never wavered throughout his long career as a bookseller and publisher.

After graduating from Harvard, Tuttle enlisted in the military and in 1945 was sent to Tokyo to work on General Douglas MacArthur's staff. He was tasked with helping to revive the Japanese publishing industry, which had been utterly devastated by the war. When his tour of duty was completed, he left the military, married a talented and beautiful singer, Reiko Chiba, and in 1948 began several successful business ventures.

To his astonishment, Tuttle discovered that postwar Tokyo was actually a book-lover's paradise. He befriended dealers in the Kanda district and began supplying rare Japanese editions to American libraries. He also imported American books to sell to the thousands of GIs stationed in Japan. By 1949, Tuttle's business was thriving, and he opened Tokyo's very first English-language bookstore in the Takashimaya Department Store in Nihonbashi, to great success. Two years later, he began publishing books to fulfill the growing interest of foreigners in all things Asian.

Though a westerner, Tuttle was hugely instrumental in bringing a knowledge of Japan and Asia to a world hungry for information about the East. By the time of his death in 1993, he had published over 6,000 books on Asian culture, history and art—a legacy honored by Emperor Hirohito in 1983 with the "Order of the Sacred Treasure," the highest honor Japan can bestow upon a non-Japanese.

The Tuttle company today maintains an active backlist of some 1,500 titles, many of which have been continuously in print since the 1950s and 1960s—a great testament to Charles Tuttle's skill as a publisher. More than 60 years after its founding, Tuttle Publishing is more active today than at any time in its history, still inspired by Charles Tuttle's core mission—to publish fine books to span the East and West and provide a greater understanding of each.

振袖
たか